Soul Source

To Cassandra,
Share my story
pg 13

Soul Source

23 Soulful Stories of Women
Who Relied on God During Difficult Times

CHERYL POLOTE-WILLIAMSON

SOUL SOURCE
Published by Purposely Created Publishing Group™
Copyright © 2017 Cheryl Polote-Williamson
All rights reserved.

No part of this book may be reproduced, distributed or transmitted in any form by any means, graphics, electronics, or mechanical, including photocopy, recording, taping, or by any information storage or retrieval system, without permission in writing from the publisher, except in the case of reprints in the context of reviews, quotes, or references.

Printed in the United States of America

ISBN: 978-1-947054-29-5

Special discounts are available on bulk quantity purchases by book clubs, associations and special interest groups. For details email:
sales@publishyourgift.com
or call (888) 949-6228.

For information logon to:
www.PublishYourGift.com

This book is dedicated to every woman
who has come to the realization that
God is her soul source.

Table of Contents

Acknowledgments xi

Embracing Love Through Faith
Dawn Baldwin Gibson 1

Distractions Are Not an Option for Failure
Roz Knighten-Warfield 13

Fear Don't Live Here Anymore
Redina Thorpe Thomas 25

My Mother's Keeper (Not All It's Cracked Up To Be)
Tneshela Boyd-Jones 37

My Joy Is Knowing My True Identity
Donna Hicks Izzard 49

A Reflection of Me
Bonita Patton-Loggins 57

A Reason for Me to Be
Tilda Whitaker 71

Remove You So GOD Can Shine Through
Becky Carter 85

In My Sight
Tabitha Wright-Polote 97

Major Depressive Disorder: It's a Journey, Not a Destination
Venessa D. Abram 107

Blocked Broken Blessed
Shawna D. Brackens 119

Seed of My Father
Taneisha Mitchell 131

Facing Grief with God's Grace
Kim Francis 143

Forgiveness Gave Me the Power to Live and Love Completely
Denise Polote-Kelly 155

God Blessed Me with the Desire of My Heart...Now What?
Alexandria L. Barlowe 165

It Starts With Me
Deandra D. Pritchett 175

Out of Darkness and Into the Light
Yolanda Williams 185

Loss and Rejection: That Stuff Challenges Your Faith
Regina M. Poole 197

Pray Without Ceasing
Pethral Daniels 205

God Set Me F.R.E.E.
Sonya A. McKinzie 217

Birthing My Source to Live Through the Power of God
M. Nichole Peters 229

Where Does Your Confidence Lie?
Kim Renee Samuels 241

God Will Give You Beauty for Ashes
Doretta Gadsden, RN 251

About the Authors 263
Sources 290

Acknowledgments

The Lord is my light and salvation whom I shall fear. I give all praise and honor to the Author and Finisher of my faith. I stand in awe by how You continue to bless me in so many ways.

To my love and partner in life, my husband, Russell M. Williamson: Words cannot express my level of gratitude for your support, your love, and your love for God. Twenty-five years later, I still say, "Yes!" I love you.

To my awesome children, Russ Jr., Lauren, and Courtney: I am so honored that you call me Mom! I am even more blessed that I get to be a grandmother to baby Leah. My heart leaps for each of you. I am a better person just by knowing you. I love you with my whole heart.

Mom and Dad: Thank you for teaching me how to love, serve, and honor God. Your support and blessings mean so much to me.

To my siblings, family, and extended family: I simply say, "Thank you!" I love all of you so much.

To my friends who know exactly who they are because our bond runs deep and long: Thank you for being everything I need when I need it. I love you.

Sincere thanks to the Green and Polote families.

Special thanks to the Blessings, Business and Collaboration Facebook Group that continues to grow and allows me to pour into thousands each day. Thanks to those who assist me in business, publisher Tieshena Davis, and the Cheryl Polote Williamson team members, Pamela Eno and Shani McIlwain.

Embracing Love Through Faith

DAWN BALDWIN GIBSON

Delight thyself also in the Lord: and he shall give thee the desires of thine heart.
Commit thy way unto the Lord; trust also in him; and he shall bring it to pass.

—Psalm 37:4-5

And being fully persuaded that, what he had promised, he was able also to perform.

—Romans 4:21

My father died when I was four-years-old. He was diagnosed with pancreatic cancer in January of 1975. Four months later, he was gone. It happened so quickly that there was really no time to process. I was what many call a "daddy's girl." I remember riding in the back of the station wagon as we drove to the bike store down the road from where we lived. Looking up in the store, I always yearned for one of those beautiful bicycles on the shelves above.

When he passed, everything all came and went so quickly. My mom decided not to remarry, dedicating herself to working and providing for our family. She made sure I had the best experiences that I could be afforded.

As I grew in age, I yearned for my daddy's love and looked in so many of the wrong places, especially in my choice of men. More often than not, I chose men who were domineering, demeaning, and possessive. I rationalized that this was how love was shown to me. Many of the men I chose had a way of diminishing my ability to shine—they mocked my accomplishments and belittled my achievements. I have always been a hard worker; I could not have been anything else having watched my mom work so hard to make a good living for me.

It was after my last serious relationship that turned violent that I knew I had to make a change. The verbal and emotional abuse was too much, and the impact it was having on my then nine-year-old son was enough to signal my need to leave that situation. I realized I had to make some significant changes in my life. The first was how I saw myself. My continued selection of men said more about my own unresolved issues than anything about them, who I gave permission to treat me and handle my spirit the way they did.

I began with prayer. After I abandoned that last relationship and returned home with my son, I knew I could never go back to the life I lived in that situation. I asked God, "What was I doing wrong? Why couldn't a man love me for me? Why couldn't he appreciate who He had made me to be? Why did I, time after time, continue to draw the same spirit of man? Because whether African-American, Hispanic, or Caucasian...the spirit was always the same."

I listened and waited. I had always dreamed of having my own family. I wanted a husband who first loved God, then me, and who I loved, knowing we were in it to win it. My prayers were different this time because I did not just talk, complain, or whine. I listened and joined my prayer with reading God's word.

I stopped. I stopped dating. For nearly three years, I learned from the lessons of my past. I went back and looked at each failed relationship and allowed the Holy Spirit to sever the soul ties that had been created. I further allowed the Holy Spirit to open the eyes of my heart to discern what had led me to those encounters. I needed to see what I was missing. What I came to see is, over and over again, was that I was choosing men who had tendencies like my father.

My mother is a smart, strong and independent woman, and there is no doubt she raised the same type of daughter. I came to realize that there were many issues my father had as a boy that grew up in him and eventually manifested in our family. I could now see that some trips we took to the bicycle shop happened after arguments he had with my mom, or worse, after he was abusive towards her. Those secret issues caused me to put a happy face on during a very dark period in my family's life. Still, these reflections had inevitably become embedded in my memory. They played out through my repeated attempts to absolve them through seeking men who fit my daddy's pattern.

During the three years of, what I called "my holding pattern," I dealt with me. I began to not only pray and study God's word but to commit His word to memory. I read particular passages over and over again, and wrote them in notebooks or on index cards. One of the first scriptures I nestled into my heart was from Psalm 37. One in particular, verse 25, I remember my maternal grandmother would often say: "I have been young, and now am old; yet have I not seen the righteous forsaken, nor his seed begging bread." It was a hallmark verse she lived by and taught on the farm that she and my granddaddy owned. But, verses 4 and 5 really sealed God's promise to me. I also went back to verse 3 to learn what it was that I had to add to my delighting in the Lord. Verse 3 reads, "Trust in the LORD, and do good; so shalt thou dwell in the land, and verily thou shalt be fed."

God began to download very specific instructions that made me deal not only with my father's death but also with the impact of a same-sex molestation that I had endured as a child. There were wounds and injuries that could not be seen by the human eye that required soul work and healing. In fact, all God was moving me toward, I could not see. But by trusting in Him, I was able to have faith that His plan was right for my life. The Lord began to move me toward building a home for my son and me. I could not understand this at the time because I thought the building of a home would be done with a husband; I believed I did not have the money or the ability to make this happen. However, God lead me to my financer and my builder who created the plan for our home. I began to listen to what God was saying and be moved by where He was leading. I still remember that early Monday morning in October 2004 when the first trucks with sand came to build up the lot. It was an incredible feeling.

To honor my blessings and to focus on my goals and myself, I remained faithful to the three years of not dating and did not entertain invites. I waited on God. I remained active in my church and community. I served and worked three to four teaching jobs. I was motivated, knowing what God's promises would be fulfilled. So, as January 2005 approached, I sought God for direction in the new year. Even though the house was nearly three months into being built, God was not signaling directions for any new love, which was still my heart's desire.

I was in my home church the first Sunday of 2005. I sat preparing for the second hymn, and I heard the quiet prompting of the Holy Spirit telling me to get up and go to the church around the corner. "What?" I thought. But still, I responded. My son and I left and went to the church around the corner and waited for more instructions. There were none until after service: I was to go to another church out of town and to continue attending this new church thereafter. I was obedient. I was learning to trust God even when I could not trace Him.

Toward the end of that month, as I saw our home near completion, I conversed with my builder and his wife. As I was preparing to leave, I thanked him for all he had done on the house and said (and I do not know why I said it), "One day, I will be talking with the President about this house."

His wife laughed; the builder did not. As I got ready to laugh, I heard the Holy Spirit say to me, "Is anything too hard for God?" Incredibly, in less than two weeks, I was sitting next to the President of the United States, discussing the new house at a town hall meeting. It started with an e-mail from a woman who had interviewed my son at a political rally. She had been so impressed by him that she wanted to stay in touch, so we exchanged business cards. Two years later, she was now working with a political party and had heard that the President was coming to North Carolina. She remembered us and asked in the e-mail if we would be interested in meeting the President Obama.

As the emails and conversations continued, I began "interviewing" to be a part of the President's town hall meeting. One afternoon, I came in my office and had a call from the switchboard operator stating that the White House was on hold to talk with me. They had completed my background check and invited my family to come to Raleigh to meet the President. The town hall meeting was to discuss the topic of social security. However, the coordinator for the town hall event shared that, after Mr. Obama read my bio, he wanted to speak with me about the new house I was building since home ownership was important to him.

I could not believe it. After that conversation, I called my builder and relayed to him what the President's staff had shared. I reminded him of the word that God had given me and he began to say, "I have to see this." The town hall meeting was broadcast live on numerous media outlets throughout the nation. I was seated next to the President and, when he introduced me, he asked about my brand new home. There it was: The fulfillment of God's word. That was a testament to the fact that God was working on my behalf in ways I could not imagine.

A few months went by, and I was still at the new church. A young man named Anthony, quite handsome I might add, inquired about my son being a part of the floor workers' ministry. I agreed and nothing more was said until, one day, we started a general conversation that lasted several hours. I began to realize that, when I was in church, I looked forward to seeing him and enjoyed when he shared his life story in Bible Study. When he asked me to hang out, I was reluctant at first, but we ended up picking up some musical instruments at a church together. On the way back, we stopped for lunch where he made the declaration that he wanted to court me to be his wife. I was shocked and stunned and immediately thought, "Wow, that was a good line." Still, I did not say much to him because I did not know what to make of his statement.

I waited. I prayed and prayed, and waited for God to speak to me. I wanted to embrace this newfound love that was happening in my life, but I needed God to speak. So I waited. Then one Sunday, I was in church when my pastor's wife began ministering through song, and I heard the word "homosexuality." I opened my eyes immediately. I continued to pray and I heard the word again. This time I opened my eyes again, and there he was, sitting two pews in front of me: Anthony. I said in my spirit, "No, not him." And the Holy Spirit revealed, "It was his past."

I took several days to digest what had been revealed. I knew my own struggles and questions with my sexuality, having been molested as a child by a female. The following Sunday during worship, the Holy Spirit shared that Anthony's heart would be mine and that we had more in common than I realized, including being molested by same-sex perpetrators. I was glad the Lord was speaking to me; still, I was very guarded from all the things that I had endured in past relationships, even though I had severed those soul ties.

Ten weeks after our courtship started, Anthony and I were married. Yes, on a beautiful Tuesday afternoon in November 2005. We met at the Justice of the Peace and were united in holy matrimony. I love that I embraced love, but what I had to realize is that our faith in God enabled us and continues to enable us to embrace our love and endure.

Our love produced more love: Hannah Elizabeth. I had been told repeatedly that I could not get pregnant because I had battled fibroids for years. They were so large at times that I looked like I was ten-weeks pregnant. But in April 2006, I found out I was eight-weeks pregnant. We were elated because God had performed a miracle beyond words. We began to make preparations for our new addition, but within weeks, I was put on bed rest due to degenerating fibroids competing for space with Hannah. I was in excruciating pain. However, it was bearable knowing that this beautiful gift was an expression of our family's love, growing healthy every day. I once again returned to memorizing the word and staying in tune with the Holy Spirit.

As the days continued to move forward, the anticipation for Hannah's arrival grew. On the evening of Thursday, July 20, I began to experience constant and severe pain. Although I had been in the emergency room that very day, I had no idea that what was occurring was not the typical pain from degenerating fibroids, but pre-mature labor. Earlier that night, my husband and son had pampered me and made sure I was getting plenty of rest. Some parts of the evening are still a blur but other parts are crystal clear.

I had drifted off to sleep around 10:30 pm after Bible Study with Anthony. My sleep world was quite active with dreams that seemed to center around my mom and I going to our family houses to do the census. The dreams ended with my maternal grandmother, who had been deceased for nearly twenty years, coming and taking Hannah from me. I was very close to my grandma, who was such a major part of the love source in my life. Even when Alzheimer's had begun to set in, she always shared love. So, for her to come to me in a dream and ask to care for Hannah—even though I understood what it meant for her to take my baby, I never worried.

When I awoke from the dream, I was in full labor—without really knowing what was happening, I called my mom, who called my Uncle Wilkie, her brother who lived on the family farm. My uncle said to call the paramedics. Unbeknownst to me, Hannah was on her way. Within minutes of arriving in the hospital, she was here, our beautiful baby girl, the little miracle baby my husband and I had awaited. She was so very precious to all, and we saw the distinct features of our little angel. Her face seemed like it was imprinted from her father, while she had my dark complexion and thick, silky hair. As we held her, we understood she was leaving us, and soon after, she was gone. Nothing at all can prepare you for the loss of a child.

The death of a child can be devastating on a marriage, especially when it is of a young one. After our baby's death, my husband and I tried to move on with life but it was hard. We had this room in our home that had already taken shape into a beautiful nursery. It now felt empty and cold. We began to turn our grief on each other through anger and hurt. We decided to separate a few weeks after Hannah's funeral. We began to work on divorce as we questioned God on why we were suffering so much grief and pain.

It was during this time that I could not cope any longer and decided to join my daughter in heaven by taking a bottle of pills. My mother found me, and I was hospitalized for several days. I was not only battling the loss of our beloved Hannah Elizabeth but also postpartum depression. My husband returned and we immediately began counseling. It was a difficult time; coping and processing was hard but I once again confirmed was that embracing love requires faith in God.

Love comes again. Over the next months, I leaned more and more on my faith and the new reality of having lost a child. My husband and I discussed whether to try again and, due to continuing issues with fibroids, we said no. So then, we decided to start the adoption process. It was several months into classes, home visits, and inspections that we learned of a little girl who had been badly beaten and was in desperate need of a good home. We were there. Given my background in education and child maltreatment and my husband's background in mental health, Kaitlyn was placed with us. God works in ways we cannot imagine. All the love that God had placed in our hearts for Hannah was being prepared for Kaitlyn. His ways are beyond our ways.

Our faith strengthened. Those years of preparation and my holding pattern were necessary for the life situations my family and I would face. Even through the loss of our child and subsequent trials, we have endured. God has matured my faith to hear Him even more.

In February of 2010, my husband and I were getting ready to check out at Target when the Holy Spirit prompted me to go back and pick up some low-dose aspirins. I told my husband, and he immediately said, "Let's get them." It would be four months later, on a Monday morning, that my husband would feel chest and arm pain signaling the onset of a massive heart attack. The next day it was determined he would have to undergo a quadruple bypass. But his doctor stated later that it was the low-dose aspirin that preserved his life until we reached the hospital. Through it all, God strengthened not only my faith but also ours as a family, and we continue to embrace the love that God has given to us.

And love now endures through Peletah. Twelve years later, I am still grateful to God for His love and the love He has blessed me with through my husband. Seven years into our marriage, God revealed that we would birth a church called Peletah, one that loves God and loves His people. Peletah is the Hebrew word for "deliverance;" through that deliverance comes the birthing of the gifts and talents that God placed in us to do His work in the earth realm.

Five years into this work where Anthony and I are pastors, we have seen people's lives transformed and families strengthened through the love and grace of Jesus Christ. Communities are impacted through the ministry for the Kingdom. We do outreach work with a remnant (another meaning of Peletah) that has seen more than thirty thousand people fed in four years; summits on poverty, racial reconciliation, and trauma informed care; grant-funded summer camps for kids at no cost to the parents; and a community farmers market.

I had no idea that those prayers, that time invested in God's word, and His cleansing of my emotional and mental clutter during that three year period was preparing my life for the destiny that He had ordained for me. He has truly gifted me with the desires of my heart and, for that, I am so very grateful. I am fully convinced that He has even more in store and I am wholeheartedly holding onto Romans 4, which declares, "And being fully persuaded that, what he had promised, he was able also to perform."

Distractions Are Not an Option for Failure

ROZ KNIGHTEN-WARFIELD

"He restores my soul; He guides me in the paths of righteousness for His name's sake."

—Psalms 23:3

Well, You Sing Well

There is a photograph of a two-year-old, sitting at a piano, hands in perfect position on the keyboard, and mouth open wide with a slight hint of a smile. She is looking over her shoulder, her shiny face covered with a nickel portion of good old Vaseline. She is nicely dressed in a sleeveless summer midriff top with coordinating shorts, ruffled socks, and blaring white tennis shoes. She has tight curled bangs and two twisted pigtails, and she is ready for a day of excitement. This toddler is me.

Whenever I see this photo, I run my fingers over the faded signage on the picture and close my eyes to activate a soul connection with my mommie. Oh, how I miss her! I open my eyes to an explosion of warm memories and read what I have now memorized by heart, what she wrote diagonally on the right corner of the picture: "We thought you'd play the piano. Well, you sing well."

That picture was taken in 1962. I was my parents' firstborn who successfully fulfilled three trimesters and entered the world, healthy and content. I was a miracle baby and a happy child indeed. Life was perfect with mommie at home. I knew no other way. She changed my clothing multiple times a day like I was a prized chocolate porcelain baby doll. She sewed beautiful dresses and playtime outfits that looked like stock photography for a 1960's version of The Children's Place. Mommie was adorable, attentive, and available at all times. She was my protector and provider. What more could a child ask for?

I never imagined a day without mommie. My little mind always knew she would be there for eternity. If I had had my way and resources as a child, she would have been honored everyday for her unconditional love that appeared to be the epitome of Galatians 5:22-23, which declares that the fruit of the Spirit is love, joy, peace, patience, kindness, goodness, gentleness, and self-control. I remember mommie's puckered up Vaseline lips that kissed all over her face while my petite hands embraced her cheeks and, without a shadow of doubt, she knew that she was loved, appreciated, celebrated, and valued. Those memories are fond and priceless.

> **Lesson One:** Be grateful for your mother and father, and appreciate their leadership, love, protection, provision, and downfalls. Those attributes will come in good use when you least expect life's curve balls.

Defiant, Depressed, and Distant

We were a middle-class military family. My daddy was an officer in the Air Force and mommie was a stay-at-home-administrator aka stay-at-home mom. Keep in mind, mommie also did some time in the Air Force, but had to take leave due to her pregnancies. I mention this because she kept a tight ship at home: You could bounce quarters off the beds she made up and it was always as though she was still enlisted on active duty for Operation Child Care.

Our life appeared to be a happily-ever-after fairytale. I played in my own back yard and all the neighborhood children came to our home, which was mommie's secret service way of keeping an eye on her assignments of duty. We enjoyed summertime vacations, attended church, had fabulous lobster boils, and much more. Life appeared to be grand.

But this lifestyle soon came to a screeching halt. There was a shift and, for reasons that were unclear to a child, Mommie was no longer my personalized stay-at-home mom. She suddenly entered the rat race known as Corporate America and began to push through tight-ended days that took on new transformations. What was happening? My world crumbled right before my eyes and I no longer had desires to sing and play the piano. I became defiant, depressed, and distant at age six. This once-happy first grader no longer smiled and her soul ached for mommie's constant availability. There was also a tsunami of tension between mommie and daddy, but they continued to press, push, and maintain monthly dues for social events.

Early morning activities in bitter-cold darkness and rage made us an assembly line of frustration. This season presented a different daily routine for my little sister and me: Being transported to school and dropped off at Big Mama's House, the new care provider. Big Mama and her family were no strangers—we all actually attended the same church and she had a daycare center in her homestead. Her center was not certified with today's credentials and met no standards. I kicked and screamed every time we had to be dropped off and was filled with delight when mommie picked us up.

My life went from *Leave it to Beaver* to a reality show of nightmares. I resented that fact that we had to be put in other people's care and grew angrier at my mommie and daddy. I still did not understand why mommie was displaced from Operation Child Care; her job was at home, but no one seemed to acknowledge or talk about the white elephant of discomfort. I knew deep in my soul that no one in this entire world could take care of us like General Mommie could. It was her honor, integrity, respect, and love—she never missed a beat.

Lesson Two: Don't get lost in hopeless encounters. Find your light in darkness and seek wise greatness in every endeavor.

Indecent Acts

Finally becoming accustomed to the drop-offs at Big Mama's house, I began to force myself to feel a sense of peace and optimism for when my mommie would pick us up every day. It became a game of empowerment and relief. I began to play again and enjoy the other children who too were forced into this mystery prison of Big Mama's Day Care. Mommie, upon pick up, began to notice that I was much calmer. Weeks passed by and I saw that she was much more at ease.

But my newfound peace ran into mass destruction that started off with tickling and riding on the back of the neck of a big, burly guy who had facial hair in patches and was larger than most of the adults who stepped foot into Big Mama's Day Care. Yes, there was laughter, but that was before I realized what was going on: I was in a closed door room with Big Mama's thirteen-year-old boy Bray aka the Babysitter's Son. The indecent acts of molestation took place.

Bray would first stuff candy in my mouth and tickle me, speaking with demanding tones that "all kids liked candy." My laugh would transition into choking on sugarbabies, trying to avoid swallowing so I could breathe through Bray's enormous hand that covered my eyes and nose. Little did I know that my mouth full of candy would act like a stuffed sock and muffle my sounds. No one could hear my silent screams. Meanwhile, a sugar high had me dizzy, nauseated, and out of sorts. He constantly repeated, "Do not tell or else."

Bray looked like a gruff country hillbilly who had aged prematurely. His body frame was at least twice my daddy's and, because of that, I believed that he would kill my mommie and daddy, and my sister and I would become foster children without parents. I also didn't want him to bother my little sister. How could this be happening to a child and no adult be aware of the hideous act? My thoughts became even more stagnated and lifeless when I realized that Big Mama knew what was happening. She became mean and callous towards me and I grew faint, weary, and lost for hope. My earth began to shatter.

Still to this day, I cringe for moms who have to drop off their children with others. Thoughts of molestation always creep up in my soul and get the best of my scarred memories. Mommie started to take me to doctors because I fell into a deep dark hole of depression. She did not understand what had happened to her gleeful, precious little girl. Doctors put the depression on growing pains. What could I say? I would not tell for fear of Bray killing my parents.

Meanwhile, his demonic acts continued. I was hurt, angry, belittled, and filled with fear, even though I had not been educated that this was wrong. I knew deep down in my soul that I did not deserve my childhood to be stripped away. Time after time, he would start tickling me, present the candy, and before I knew anything, his hands were over my eyes and nose and his selfish acts were happening all over again. Why did I not have the courage or boldness to tell? How could I believe the lie? Angry and dismayed with myself, I felt like damaged goods and no longer knew the happy child that was in the picture, playing the piano and singing with her heart's content.

Lesson Three: No matter what, be bold when wrong stares you in the face. Shout out for Jesus. He will come rescue you.

"The Lord is good. When trouble comes he is a strong refuge."
—Nahum 1:7

Unhealthy Emotions

Silent frustrations captured me. I was a kid who was bullied and tormented, and for what reason? Soon, I became a people pleaser and longed for friends who could be trusted, but apparently, I was wearing a sign on my forehead and back that read, "Treat me wrongly." I was mad at God and asked every moment, "Why did you let this happen to me? How could you, Lord?" There were days that I was defiant, depressed and distant, but guess what? I was the only one who knew of my pain. I operated like a functioning alcoholic—the individual who makes it on time to work to hide his addiction and not lose his job. I operated so others could not figure out my flaws. I stayed steps ahead to avoid building up true friendships. I was not trusting, but you would never know it because I kept myself busy to avoid the pain of seeing myself as damaged goods.

Elementary led to middle school and middle school led to high school. I led a promiscuous teen lifestyle in which I teased and got any male figure. On several occasions, this manner of action almost cost me my life. I was playing

Russian roulette with my life because I was hurt and keeping secrets of the enemy's agendas that had my life spiraling downward. Soon, I was twenty-six and had still not told a soul about my trauma.

As a young adult, I continued to live a double life of despair, going to church by day and partying at night. The last time, I almost got killed and was raped for trying to play games. A friend came over and assisted me and shared her story which was parallel to mine; she continued on to share that, while many of the wrongdoings in my life were not my fault, I was still responsible for the choices and decisions I made. Her name was Starris and she saved my life that night. I repented, asked God for forgiveness, and started going to counseling to detox my tormented battlefield of a mind.

Counseling: A giant journey was at hand for emotional healing. But for physical healing, I entered a love affair with food and gained a lot of weight, and I also indulged in smoking marijuana. My makeup, character, and identity were all being challenged because I was molested as a child. Trying to camouflage the hurt as an adult was a different cycle of craziness that demanded various forms of coping. Nevertheless, I had to trust in God, affirm myself, and realize that Rome was not built in one day. The Original Big Daddy, the Lord, only wants the best for His daughter.

> **Lesson Four:** God wants the best for you. You are a child of the Most High King. Get in His presence at every opportunity and have conversations with Daddy. He loves you! His arms are open wide to hug you!

It's Time to Trust

It's time to trust, believe and respect the soul source of my life. The muckidy yuck of thoughts no longer reign as lead drummer. It's a new day to consider myself free from being a victim and sing and shout victory is mine. I started believing in myself again. I accepted that I could not do it by myself. I had to begin exercising and doing my homework to soar like an eagle and stop clucking around like a chicken.

I started listening to the constructive voices of transformation. I also flooded my vocabulary with words that told me I am wonderful, victorious, smart, and a giver at heart. I was reminded that the Devil was purposely trying to derail me and that he was pissed off that I had been realigned to my born again self. I was still responsible for choices and actions and had to embrace God as my coach.

Acknowledging responsibility began a journey of owning my worth and releasing the label of damaged goods. Consistency is a devised plan of action to erode old habits and fashion new habits. We were born with success in our DNA. The D is for discovery, the N is for nurture and the A is for activate. God is our Refuge and Strength [mighty *and* impenetrable to temptation], a very present *and* well-proved help in trouble. Psalm 46:1 AMPC

I began reading again and realized how dormant my mind had been. Self-care, self-love, self-respect, and self-commitment are very important. One of my coaches said the other day, "Be committed to the commitment of your yes." Those words hit me like a ton of bricks. It's time to trust yourself and know how great you are and the world is waiting for you. Someone needs to know your story and it will set them free.

If you are reading this, it's time to come out of the darkness into the Son-light of Jesus's love. If you don't have a relationship with Jesus Christ, you can accept him right now as your Lord and Savior, and confess all the wrong doings and choices of your life.

Relational Currency

Words can feed your soul. They can empower, equip, and elevate a broken spirit to a place of being whole, fit, and well. My transformation would not have happened without the support of others. Relational currency deals with the engagement of two or more people communicating in harmony to walk out a goal, vision, idea, or thought. It is also respecting others' uniqueness without disrespecting their perspective in any way.

To transform and renew your mind, you must also stop lower nature thinking that causes negativity and makes intentional love encounters, starting with yourself. The greatest help manual is the Bible and, if we meditate on the word day and night and read out loud, a change will come. The power of reading is to remind you that you are a wordsmith of the Lord and you can realign your destiny by the power of words. Know that you are a skilled user of God's words and decree and you declare your newness in Christ.

It is possible to dismiss the pain of your past and not allow distractions to be an option for failure, quitting, or giving up. Find a support tribe who will keep you accountable and catapult you to the next level. Ask for strength, endurance, and courage and be the light that Daddy says you are in the kingdom.

Some affirmations for you to get started:
I am loved with an everlasting love (Jeremiah 31:3).
I am free of shame and condemnation (Romans 8:1).
I can do all things through Christ (Philippians 4:13).
I have been called by God (2 Timothy 1:9).
I am beloved and chosen of God (Colossians 3:12).
I am God's workmanship (Ephesians 2:10).

My True Soul Source

It is not by mistake that Cheryl Polote-Williamson handpicked twenty-three women to create a mosaic of transparencies to share with other women who need to be catapulted out of darkness into the great light. I thank you for this opportunity.

Ladies who are survivors of childhood molestation, it's time to ask God, "What is my work of art?" Your soul source is the Original Big Daddy. He loves you deeply and you were created for His glory. You are loved, appreciated, celebrated, and valued! God is your true source and He longs for you to utilize your resources and operate as His beloved daughter.

Lesson Five: For grace and His never-ending mercy!

Fear Don't Live Here Anymore

REDINA THORPE THOMAS

*Don't be afraid of your fears. They're not there to scare you.
They're there to let you know that something is worth it.*

—C. JoyBell

One early morning on a drizzly January day in 1985, I was driving during the height of traffic in downtown Savannah. I remember a loud sound that resonated in my tympanic membrane—a sound like cymbals in an orchestra. As I began to get my bearings, I realized I had been rear-ended, and my vehicle had catapulted to the opposite end of Bay Street. My first response was fear. I had just dropped my daughter off at the babysitter, which was a huge blessing since I knew that she was not harmed—she would have been in the backseat and killed instantly.

I didn't realize at the time that I would become indestructible like an eagle, one who knows when a storm is approaching. The eagle waits for the winds to come, and though it does not escape the storm, it is able to use the winds and rain to lift its body even higher, above the cloud. My accident turned out to be symbolic: It was only the calm before the real storm that would rage on my life in the next five years to come.

After the accident, my first response was to call my husband to let him know that I had been in an accident. I informed him that I was checked by emergency medical services who advised me to go to the hospital for further testing. For the first few days, I was in pain due to my neck and back injury. My husband was attentive and supportive during the beginning phase of my accident, getting my prescriptions and neck brace. I could not report to work due to my injuries, so I contacted my school where I was a paraprofessional at the time. My assistant principal told me to contact him daily about my condition and that he would secure a substitute each day as needed. In the days to come, I would faithfully contact my assistant principal (AP) each morning as I had been instructed.

My husband was often somewhere nearby, listening to these phone conversations. After I would get off the phone, he would make inappropriate remarks such as, "That must be your boyfriend. You must be sleeping with him." I would, of course, defend my honor, self-dignity, and respect by assuring him that he was the only man I had ever been with and that his comments were absolutely absurd and disrespectful. One day, he came home after work and entered the den with my home phone in his hand. He started dialing a number on my phone. He said, "I'm going to see what man you've been calling."

I watched in horror because I could hear the voice of the man on the line. It was my AP. My husband accused him of seeing his wife and started cursing him out. My AP tried to explain to him that it was my responsibility to contact the school about my condition on a daily basis, but my husband did not want to hear this. I was embarrassed and thought I could never set my foot back into the building after what just transpired. I did call and apologize for my husband's actions later; in that moment, he was like a raging bull.

After he got off the phone, it was my turn to feel the wrath. He started arguing and calling me a whore and a no-good bitch, which he did on numerous occasions. The more I tried to defend my honor, the angrier he became. The next thing I knew, he started punching me repeatedly in my left arm, over twenty times with excessive force. I ran across the street to a trucking company to seek refuge.

I told the trucking company's supervisor that my husband and I were arguing and that he had punched my arm. They immediately called the police and an ambulance. The paramedics wanted to take me to the hospital, which I refused at first because, as is the case with many victims of domestic violence, I wanted to protect my abuser and was extremely fearful of him.

I called my mom who was at work, and she got off her job and met me at the hospital. I stopped revealing the truth, but she knew in her gut what had happened. She asked the nurse to talk to me and see if I would confide in her, but I still would not tell my side of the story. The doctor then entered the room, trying to ask more questions about the incident, but I still held tight to this secret and continued to protect my husband. I left the hospital with a bruised collarbone.

My life would continue to be plagued with fear. Fear has always been my crippling factor, and that is why I constantly ask God to remove my giants. I did not always recognize fear as my giant, but once I started seeking Him, He revealed it to me. He now allows me to pray and seek his guidance for total restoration.

Paradigm of Fear

I was always an extremely shy girl and rarely talked in school. I came from a strict upbringing and there was an unspoken demand to be perfect, which placed pressure on both my older brother and me. With that being said, my childhood was great. My mom stayed at home for the most part and was always visible and available for my friends and me; my dad was a commercial fisherman in the early seventies who had done extremely well for an African American man, considering the era. It was all well until I soon began sneaking out to see a young man who later became my husband, even though I was forbidden to see him or take company at all.

The abuse and betrayal began while I was dating my husband. He was eighteen and I was only fifteen when we started seeing each other. He would shower me with gifts and, because I was extremely naïve, I did not have a clue about intimacy. I had no idea that, years later, my life would be crippled with abuse, lies, and deceit. I saw a true glimpse of this man when he punched me in my chest so hard that I could not breathe and all he did was laugh while I tried to catch my breath. The essence of my very existence was being taken away at the hands of this man. I soon left and stayed with my aunt for two weeks until he razzled and dazzled me right back into the pits of hell. This became a continuous cycle.

In hindsight, I was too young to get married at the age of nineteen. I did not really know the man I was married to or myself. Instead, this should have been a time to begin my life by first taking care of myself. I wanted a man like my father who was kind and loving. As a young woman, you hope to fall in love and live out that fairy tale dream, but my life was a far cry from a storybook dream. It continued to be a paradigm of intimidation tactics, fear, and abuse throughout each of my pregnancies. I was slapped and punched repeatedly and went into early labor due to abuse and stress. I was stripped of my dignity and self-respect at the hands of a man.

My mother, who was my backbone, told me I could not come back home because I kept repeating the same behavior over and over again; so, I eventually went to a safe home for battered women and sought counseling for the situation in my home. This experience was even more frightening because I was not like the other women in the shelter, many of whom were addicts and prostitutes. But I soon realized our common thread: Abuse and fear. After some soul searching, I realized my failed relationship did not work because of my trust in man and not God, who would lead and guide my way. I was heartbroken each time a relationship ended, thinking it was the right relationship, but I accepted the fact that God was making me stronger. All through the years of turmoil, He had the master plan.

The abuse that I experienced was supposed to break me, but it made me a strong independent woman. I was young, married at nineteen with limited education, and a mother to three young daughters. What made me fight hard were my girls. I was all they had for parental support and I had to show them how to grow in the Lord and that, despite our struggles, there was still a God who we must serve and trust. I knew I had to get us out of that abusive situation, for "Suffer little children to come unto me for theirs is the kingdom of heaven..." (Matthew 19:14 KJV). I realized I was indeed a victim of domestic violence and had been through a lot of trauma both physically and mentally. It was going to take a mighty move of God to put me back together again! I had to first move from a state of denial to a state of trusting and believing that God would change my circumstances, whatever they may be.

Living as a single mom with three children was an arduous task. There were times when we had very little food to eat. I had to borrow money from loan companies; at the time, I think I had a loan at every small company in the city. I made a pledge to save my children from circumstances into which they did not choose to be born. I decided to enroll them in private school and give them what my parents afforded me: An education built on both excellence and strong religious teachings. It was difficult to be a paraprofessional and raise three daughters and put them through private school. I received assistance through the Catholic dioceses of Savannah, but I still had to pay the bulk of tuition and book fees on my own. I did receive child support, but it was never consistent and I would often times have to repay loans when I would receive large sums of money due to arrearages. Huge sacrifices were made, but I do not regret any of them.

I look back and think: How did I do the things I did? I left a man who I was truly afraid of. I left a man who provided every material desire that a woman could have and gave me a certain lifestyle. Deep inside, there was still this strong, determined woman who said, "You do not deserve to be mistreated. God has a better plan for your life. Leave and don't look back." I never knew my strength until I left. My spirit is now new because God saw fit to save me and use me as a vessel.

Once my husband and I were divorced, I used my settlement to better my circumstances. My principal at the time saw potential in me to become a school leader and wrote a letter of recommendation to get me into a teaching program called Pathways to Teaching (a program for minority teachers funded by Dewitt Wallace *Reader's Digest*). I was a full-time paraprofessional by day and attended school at night. I had great support from my mom and younger brother who assisted me in caring for my children, and my parents worked hard at building a family business, which allowed me to finally have a stable place to raise my daughters and rebuild my life. I thank God for a supportive, loving, and caring family who believed in me. Thanks to hard work and the help I received, after completion of my bachelor of arts degree in English language and literature, I earned my teacher certification in middle grade English and social studies, my leadership certification, and my master's degree in education.

I can see now that God's gift shines through me in the classroom and around my students. He gave me a gift that has now enabled me to get a position as a behavior specialist. It's amazing how a seed is germinated and becomes a bud then a flower. My job consists of observing and making recommendations to improve classroom management, and working with students in small groups and through one-on-one teaching strategies to improve their behavior, which will ultimately lead to improved academic achievements. I enjoy working with the most challenging students because I know they need love and additional support. I was never the smartest student in the class, but once I found my craft, I soared like an eagle. And I know they can too. God chose me for this job because he was grooming me all along.

A teacher once told me, "Ms. Thomas, you have earned your place in heaven." People saw something in me that I did not see in myself as a survivor. I thought I had to remain humble, pleasant, and kind in spite of my past struggles, and not become a bitter woman who took my problems out on others. I wanted to hide my wounds and keep my life a secret, and I was embarrassed that I was a victim of domestic violence.

This was a flaw in my character: Trying too hard to look good for the public. Many women suffer in silence just as I did.

Tucking Fear Away and Finding God

Over a year, I kept praying and fasting. I could see myself getting stronger and stronger. I continued to pray and found myself at the altar on several Sundays during the church service, requesting prayer. It was one Sunday afternoon when Pastor Alan Dwayne O'Neal Sr. called for an altar call. I went up and felt very calm, and as pastor prayed, something came over me. I started weeping and crying and almost gasping for my breath. Overwhelmed with relief, I kept saying, "It's gone, it's gone. It's over!"

This was the second or third time that I had become emotional while at the altar or in the choir stand. God was making me a new creature. I found myself more relaxed in the church service. I had always been extremely reserved, but when the spirit of the Lord is upon you, all of that goes out the window! You don't care what people think about you. To God be the Glory!

I realized that God gave me a reasonable amount of physical beauty, which sometimes seems to be a curse. Many people look at your physical beauty and automatically conclude that, "She thinks she's all that." I've lived in this skin for many years, this light complexion and beautiful hair. I used to play down my looks for other women, but no more. God chose me to have all that I do. My beauty is not a curse and it does not define me. I am a child of God and that is what I treasure the most. My inner beauty is my best asset and a true gift from heaven.

"Do not be afraid; you will not be put to shame. Do not fear disgrace; you will not be humiliated. You will forget the shame of your youth and remember no more reproach of your widowhood. For your maker is your husband—The Lord Almighty is his name—the Holy one of Israel is your redeemer; He is called the God of all the earth."

—Isaiah 54:4

All I ever really needed was to know who was truly the head of my soul and then my life would indeed begin to change and the doors would spring open. After a series of Mr. Wrongs in my life, I believe I finally have a Mr. Right. I have prayed that God would send me a true Godly man, one who walks the walk and talks the talk, one who would personify a Christian man. Once I submitted myself totally to God's will, I was able to receive the desires of my heart. Furthermore, I want my children to have a devoted and caring man in their lives.

When the storms of life comes upon us, just like the eagle, we can and must rise above and ride the winds that create fear and doubt, until total restoration occurs and we are no longer paralyzed by them. Fear is the main force in an abused person's life, but there is strength in knowing that God is just a prayer away, even when everything is falling around you. Though I no longer fear man, I do fear God. I want to be able to spread the good news about what He will do for us, if we only trust him. When the Holy Spirit enters into our lives, it is the beginning of a new way of living. We become new creatures in Christ.

Fear don't live here anymore!

When fear becomes your best friend, remember:

- Seek God to give you discernment so that you may make wise decisions and have sound judgments
- Know your strengths and weakness—recognize and foster them

- Pray in order to gain strength in accessing the road map for your journey
- Tell someone you trust what you are experiencing
- Remember that fear is only a state of mind
- Do not doubt your gifts and talents
- It's never too late to pursue your dreams
- Develop a short term plan and begin execution
- When God is in your plan, you will succeed
- Never allow a man to take control over your thoughts
- If he hits you once, he will hit you again
- Always have an escape plan
- Never be afraid to tell someone
- Save monies for your getaway plan

My Mother's Keeper
(Not All It's Cracked Up To Be)

TNESHELA BOYD-JONES

"Praise be to the Lord, who has given rest to his people Israel just as he promised. Not one word has failed on all the good promises he gave through his servant Moses."

—1 Kings 8:56

Me and my momma used to have a ball. The lady would do the craziest things to keep me laughing. Making funny faces at me while driving, sticking her tongue out and making googly eyes, Momma made every day a new adventure. Some days, we'd hike up the mountains, letting our hands graze the flowers and picking up their dewy scents; then we'd swing from branches over waterfalls like Tarzan and Jane; well, Jane and me, her ever-willing daughter.

These adventures always started off with us taking long rides down the Pacific Coast Highway, to no particular place or at least no place that I knew of. The music would play loudly, and my momma and I would sing (I sang badly), as we rolled along scenic highways of Southern California. Momma could really blow a tune and she knew it. Natalie Cole was her go-to artist. Sometimes, when I close my eyes,

I can still hear her singing "This Will Be" and "I'm Catching Hell." Momma loved all kinds of good music from Stevie Wonder to Aretha, and oh, that woman could dance her butt off. My momma was talented, artistic, ambitious, the life of any party; when she walked in, the room would pause.

Have you ever witnessed an anomaly? I mean one of those beautiful rarities found in a soul that could captivate and leave you wanting more? That was my momma. She had a presence and the undisputed style of mahogany. The fellas chased this gorgeous chocolate sister with the long, straight, flowing hair, but a good chase was all they ever got, because she always moved too fast to be caught. I was always proud when someone asked if she was my momma. She was a young—she turned eighteen a week after she gave birth to me—and looked like my older sister, and she honestly could have been. My childhood was fun because she was like my playmate. We discovered things together.

Around my thirteenth birthday, I went on my very first summer vacation to visit my Godmother and her two daughters in Detroit, Michigan, or Motown as some call it. My godmother's daughters were like my sisters, especially since I was an only child. I bonded with them since we were one, two, and three years apart. They were truly my sisters, and we got into the world of teenage mischief, blaming one another for each other's crimes. It was truly my coming-of-age movie minus the Bob Saget voiceover. Going to Bobalo Island, eating my weight in White Castle burgers, attending meet-ups at parties, talking to boys, kissing boy's at the movies, and going places we had no business going, knowing if we got caught it would be our butts—it was the most amazing two weeks I'd ever had.

After doing as much as my pre-teen body would allow, I returned to Los Angeles. I couldn't wait to see my momma. I had a fantastic time on my mini-summer vacation but I really missed her smiling face and our everyday life with a touch of adventure. However, when I got home, the energy in the air was different, and something just wasn't right. There was a man and his presence stunk of change. He began coming around regularly, and my momma's attention and time that used to be mine were now his. I was no longer the center of her world. Since I was an only child who'd grown up thinking all we had was each other, my momma and I had created what I thought was an unbreakable bond. Little did I know this man would invade our world.

A part of me didn't believe that such drastic change could occur in my two-week absence. Jealous? Yes, maybe. But seeing as though I was fourteen and starting to "smell myself," it gave me more freedom to explore and do my own thing, and Momma gave me no push back. After all, there was something new about her that she needed to discover and my being out of the way gave her that freedom.

As time passed, my freedom became strangely limited. Things were different, but I wasn't sure what it was. Suddenly, there was never money for anything. My mother started sending me to the store with IOU notes for things she wanted and couldn't afford. The embarrassment of giving that sheet of paper to the man behind the cash register weighed on me, and I looked around to see if anyone else witnessed me handing the note. I would sometimes wonder what he must have thought: "This little girl's mother don't ever have any money."

While sending me out with IOU's, my momma also started dodging the landlord. She'd send me to the door to speak to the landlord with a constructed lie she wanted me to tell. What was I supposed to do? I had the innocent face. I'm sure he thought, "A child would never say this magnitude of a lie," but I knew he could tell it wasn't the truth.

This behavior had become a norm over the next couple years: My momma, using me as a pawn in her game of deceit. Our lives changed drastically, and I began to feel like that summer plane trip sent me to another place in time, as if life had passed through some dark cloud to the Twilight Zone. There went those good ole days, and the truth of why things were different finally surfaced: I'd returned to my momma's addiction to crack cocaine. Not only was I clueless to the situation, but I also didn't understand how all this could happen over a two-week vacation. Things spiraled faster and faster out of control. My mother started disappearing for days on end and returning with no explanation, like her absence never happened. On top of that, momma and I began moving regularly and living with others.

Things were about to get even harder for her. My mother had to answer some hard questions. The family wanted to know the reasons for the disappearances and why she was financially struggling. I was a child—I had no clue what those adult conversations were about, but I was aware enough to know the family did what they could and, once they were fed up, gossip was spoken aloud in my presence when momma wasn't around. I tried to conceal my emotions as not to seem ungrateful to those who were allowing me to lay my head down in their homes, but it pissed me off and hurt my feelings. In my silence, I hid my tears. Despite what was going on, at the end of the day, that woman was my mother, and I would stand by her side.

After being evicted from our apartment, we moved in with my momma's boyfriend against my better judgment—hell, against anybody's better judgment. After all, this was the man who had gotten my mother hooked on crack and destroyed everything we had together. I hated him and every part of this idea to the point it made me sick. I was floored that my mom was so enthralled with this warped love story they'd created together. It didn't even matter to her that his home was neglected and infested with roaches. Nothing around them mattered; even worse, I didn't matter. I would find myself praying for God to hear me. How could He do nothing about what was happening to me? He is God, right? At one point, I thought that maybe I wasn't praying loud enough.

There was no way that I was going to stay in that house. I started to leave, not knowing where I was going to go. I'd leave daily and did everything possible to keep from returning to this so-called home. I would ride the bus and walk all over Los Angeles as long as possible before I would go back to that house to sleep on the sofa with the roaches. Still, I couldn't stand it for long and went back to live with friends and family, trying to hold on to some normalcy. My thought was, I'd rather sleep on a friend's couch and be hungry and cold, rather than sit and watch the shit that was happening at home and risk hating my mother forever.

I knew I was breaking in my spirit, my heart, and my understanding. All of what was happening had me latching onto anything that felt like love. I needed something to comfort me and to make me feel safe again. At age fifteen, I began to free fall into promiscuity. The feeling of someone's body pressed against mine seemed to fill the void of a mother's hug, at least for long as it was happening. But when it was over, I still felt empty. I knew what I was doing wasn't right, but I'd still put myself in a position to be sexually taken advantage of. Each and every time, I felt God tap me on my shoulder and ask, "What are you doing?" Most times I didn't even have an answer other than "What else was I supposed to do?"

Like almost every lesson to be learned, you sometimes have to hit rock bottom before you see God's light. It was in the throes of false love—boyfriends had become *my* drug—that my pain had somewhat eased. My mother and I had more in common than I thought. But the first of many breakthroughs that would pull me closer to the word of God came when I made a few visits to church with my grandmother and close friends. The Word became so evident to me—it was like I could finally hear God talking to me clearly, giving me building blocks. I wanted to be all God expected me to be; even when I was willingly putting myself in danger and sin, His approval was necessary to me. I spoke to God, begging for his forgiveness for the things I had done and His grace to fix my life, because He was the only one with the power to do so.

Some prayers were answered: My momma's boyfriend was finally no more, and we were blessed with a small one-bedroom apartment that someone had vouched for momma to get. I felt that everything was getting back on track. I was happy to see flickers of the momma that I remembered. I'd love to say that all was well and life was a crystal staircase after that, but old habits die hard and hers were not going away without a fight.

Soon after we moved in, my momma started ditching the landlord again. My dream of normalcy was going down the drain. By the time I was sixteen, I'd been through five high schools in a three-year period. I was stressed and unfocused to the point my grandma would give me Valium to calm my nerves. I refused to miss a day of school and I did everything I could to show up. I wanted to get it right. Schooling was the one thing that I felt in control of. Still, I also desperately craved stability, family love, and a mother I could be proud of—our lifestyle just wasn't designed to give me that chance.

My hopes of things returning to normal were coming to an end as I continued to pray for our situation. The enemy was hell-bent to destroy us and he did so by crushing my one mustard seed of faith: That Momma never allowed me to witness her using crack. I came home from school one day and was unable to get in, because she refused to open the door. Locked out with nowhere to go, I banged and banged on the door until she let me in. With no shame, my momma continued smoking crack with my childhood babysitter of all people. I went completely ballistic witnessing Momma delighting in her drug use. To this day, I can't forget the smell of the burning chemicals and the walls covered with black handprints from the burning soot. How dare she break the promise she made to herself to try and hide the evidence?

All of it crowded my mind and caused feelings of confusion, of helplessness, of being trapped, and of rage. All I can remember about that moment is going into the bathroom, swinging and punching at the air with my fists, silently crying and yelling out to God to help me, to free me from the madness. I wanted to be free from dreams of crack pipes chasing me and haunting me. I wanted to be free me from the worries of my mother coming up missing or being killed. I wanted to be free from the chatter and gossip, free from feeling helpless, free from the pain of feeling abandoned, and free from wishing she'd just die.

My face drowned in my hands full of tears. I flopped down onto the toilet seat, begging for God to do something. Then, in that instant, as if hypnosis had been cast on me with the snap of His fingers, God called me to attention. A focused calm came over my body. I sat there, frozen with my eyes wide open, staring at the white wall in front of me through my tear-soaked eyes; I heard God clearly speak to me, "You aren't your mother's keeper. This isn't your responsibility, and I am here for you. Put your mother and her troubles in My hands. I will bear her burdens. I need you to be whole. I need you to be the person your mother raised you to be. You are loved. I am your mother's keeper and I will never leave you." He promised that, if I walked away and trusted Him, He would make everything right again.

Once God showed me I was strong enough to walk my lone journey without momma, I loved her from afar and almost acted as if she didn't exist. The past left me with severe wounds and walls that cut off my ability to express emotions, which I'm now sharing for the first time here, with you. However, believing God's promise allowed me to look at life optimistically with affirmations and prayer. So many times, I'd feel like the pain cut too deep for me to heal or my momma would try to get too close to me, but I kept moving forward with elevated spirits to create the life of normalcy that I longed for. This was what prevented me from breaking.

I can still hear Momma calling me "Hard-Hearted Hanna." I'm not sure where she picked up that term but little did she know how my heart tightened during my thoughts of her in her absence. If she only knew how much I loved and missed her...still, I had to stay strong. I couldn't let her or myself down. There was never a decision I made through which I didn't try to make her proud; after all, we were still mother and daughter. And I could also see that she was doing everything possible to heal through the years as she struggled for her sobriety.

With no one to turn to for over twenty years, I dug deep into myself, riding on the high of God's promise. I created something out of nothing, took advantage of every opportunity allowed to me, and walked through every door opened, grinding and climbing to succeed despite my lack of education and opportunity. My goal was not only to overcome my obstacles but to prove to myself that I was capable and deserving to be just as financially viable and mentally available for my family as someone with the ideal upbringing. I never knew when to expect a call of need from my family. I was the matriarch.

In 2008, at forty-years-old, I lost everything. Who could ever forget the big bubble that burst, putting us Americans in a recession? I was laid off and unable to find employment anywhere. Unable to afford my mortgage, I had to sell both my homes. My two kids were exiting high school and off on their own journeys, while Momma was stable and sober, and we had begun communicating somewhat regularly. I had always made a point to show up during her stints with sobriety but continued keeping a safe distance.

While having a conversation with Momma, I shared my dilemma with her and ideas of trying to devise a new plan. Momma listened intently; I could hear her take a puff of her cigarette as she responded, "Well, baby, it sounds like you may need to come live with me." It was like hearing a foreign language for the first time; my husband, Jared, and I quietly tried to process what my mother said. My first thought was, "That sounds absurd." Moving back home, with my parent? Never an option I could have imagined considering. I flashed back to twenty-four years ago when I was sitting in that bathroom, being instructed by God with tear soaked hands, as He promised me He would handle our burden. Tears began to flow silently from my eyes, as my momma continued to puff on her cigarette. Could this really be?

Yes. With my hands tied and having no other options, I was able to tear down the walls built of pain—I began to love on my mother and to be loved on by her in return. Momma never had to ask for my forgiveness because my faith and hope never let her feel that I gave up on her.

Moving in with momma was a bittersweet time: It seemed that I had lost everything, but I gained a deeper understanding that I am never alone with God by my side. And I got my momma back! Even now as a divorcee and a mother of two with a great career, life still has a funny way of continuously shifting.

Your parents may not have been addicted to drugs, but you too may have gone through a situation that left you feeling lost and alone. It is in these times that, if you listen, God will redirect you so that all parties involved can find healing and sanctuary in Him. Know God hears you and is helping you weather the storms, even when you don't know he's carrying you.

Ten W.I.S.D.O.M K.E.Y.S to Embracing Love through Faith

1. **W**eary not in well doing: Do not get tired of waiting for your promise. God is faithful and He will bring it to pass.
2. **I**nvest time in the process: Nothing has an overnight fix. God's timing is perfect and, while the process may not be easy, it will most assuredly be worth it.
3. **S**ee the big picture: Take time and envision what God has spoken to you. Make a vision board and put God's word for your life into pictures.
4. **D**on't look for shortcuts: Shortcuts are always alluring, but they diminish the lesson that God wants to birth in us by going through the process.
5. **O**pen your heart when the Holy Spirit leads: Whether it is a new relationship or friendship, do not allow past hurts and injuries to cause you to be

so trapped that you miss out on worthwhile opportunities to embrace love.
6. **M**ake notes: Journal your journey. Take time to write down what you are experiencing and what God is showing you through your personal devotion time in prayer or through the Holy Scriptures.
7. **K**now that God has anointed you to win: God has purposed your life for greatness—do not ever forget that God has made you to win.
8. **E**mbrace challenges: Challenges are never easy, but they are necessary. They reveal the strength that God has placed in you.
9. **Y**ield your vessel to the One who created the vessel: God knows.
10. **S**hare your story: At the appointed time, God will allow you the opportunity and platform to share your story with those who need to hear it.

My Joy Is Knowing My True Identity

DONNA HICKS IZZARD

"His anger is but for a moment, His favor is for life; weeping may endure for a night, but joy comes in the morning."

—Psalm 30:5

What a blessing it is to know who I am and whose I am. There was a time when I could not experience that joy because I allowed myself to be filled with pain afflicted by another person. I allowed this individual to make me feel unworthy or not good enough to be loved and chosen. I often share with others that identity is the foundational core of our lives. I am filled with joy because I now know my true identity.

Some time ago, I found myself in a situation that left me wondering if God actually loved me. Lying on the floor of my sister's apartment, I asked: "How did I get here? What happened?" I thought my boyfriend loved me. He told me that he was happy that I was having his baby, his son. Why did he leave me? How did I allow this to happen to me? Why did I believe him? Here I was twenty-three years old, alone, ashamed, depressed, humiliated, seven-months pregnant, and abandoned by the father of my child. Wow, how things had changed!

I had a luxury apartment in one of the most desirable neighborhoods in New York City. I wore designer clothes. Went on trips out of the country as often as I wanted to. And was able to take my family and friends on shopping sprees. I had an amazing income and, in my mind, I had arrived. I was doing well and I did not need anyone. I was the young woman from the hood that was going to make an impact and a difference.

But the pregnancy threw me into a situation that I never saw coming. I had been the smart one, the daughter my mom had high hopes for. Yet, here I was, pregnant, no baby father, and emotionally bankrupt. Was I really going through this nightmare? I was on a life roller coaster and had no clue of how I was going to make the ride stop. Moreover, I started to hate myself, and did not want to be pregnant. I did not care about my appearance; I just wanted to get back to normalcy, which, for me, meant getting rid of the baby, terminating the pregnancy at the almost seven months.

This was a new place for me. Was I willing to stoop so low that I would get rid of my baby? Who was I? Why did I allow this man to have control over me? Was I not worthy? Was I not pretty enough? Why would God allow this to happen to me? I had all of these questions for God, but no one could give me any answers.

I worried about how people would judge me for what had happened, and dreaded the thought of them talking about me. I was humiliated beyond belief, so I stopped speaking to my friends. My family did not know how to console me since I became somebody else. I was a complete mess, the actions of another person causing me to break down completely.

Clearly, I did not know who I was. This is a story that is often told by many young women, yet I never thought it would happen to me. I remember these situations happening to my sister, her friends, and even some of my friends. But me?

My family tried to be there for me as much as possible. My sister opened up her apartment to me. Due to the fragility of my mental state, I lost everything: My job, my apartment, and my money. I was broken, financially and in spirit. But losing my identity was the most detrimental—interestingly enough, it was also what forced me to get back on track with my life. Although my boyfriend left me, God stayed with me.

We tend to obsess over what other people think of us. We go through life trying desperately to earn fame or fortune in hopes that we might be recognized. But when all is said and done, where is our real identity? People are imperfect and superficially biased. A house built on sand will only collapse. But a house built on solid ground will endure. We should base the perceptions we have of ourselves, not on the opinions of others, but on the Word of God. Knowing your identity means knowing two things: Who you are and whose you are.

> "But you are a chosen race, a royal priesthood, a holy nation, a people for his own possession, that you may proclaim the excellences of him who called you out of darkness into his marvelous light."
>
> −1 Peter 2:9

So who are you, really? The Bible has a lot to say about who we are in God's eyes. First, we are made in His image: We weren't meant to be insecure about our appearances, because God made us just the way He wanted us, and He doesn't make mistakes. Don't ever put yourself down or beat yourself up because you don't meet society's standards. The world sees beauty from the outside, but God sees beauty from the heart. On the flip side, you can't act superior to anyone else either. We should neither be insecure or arrogant, but confidently humble. Romans 12:3 says, "For by the grace given to me I say to everyone among you not to think of himself more highly than he ought to think, but to think with sober judgment, each according to the measure of faith that God has assigned." Do not trample on the rest of the world, and do not let the rest of the world trample you. We are all infinitely and equally treasured by God.

Now to the second question: Whose are you? The answer has less to do with the mind and more to do with the heart. This question is one of personal reflection and a good one to ask whenever you feel the need to gauge your relationship with God. Are you devoting yourself to the things of this world, or are you pursuing Christ with reckless abandon? If you belong to the world, you're going to get knocked down and not be able to get up. But if you belong to God, there is hope. There is hope because Jesus loved you enough to die on a cross for your sins. He saw your faults and your failures, and He wanted to save you from them before it was too late. His strength shines through your weakness. If you suffer for Christ, you are a co-heir with Him, and you will share in His glory one day. The Bible says that we are more than conquerors in Him. He who defeated death and the grave can surely defeat his own insecurities.

Now, all of this doesn't mean that there won't be hardship. Trusting in Jesus doesn't guarantee you an easy life. There will be persecution. You will probably be more hated than you would be if you followed the world. But take heart—in John 15:18, Jesus says, "If the world hates you, know that it has hated me before it hated you." Jesus suffered more than all of us. He was slaughtered and disgraced by the ones He came to save. He, the greatest of all, became the least for the sake of the world. It is our Christian duty to follow in His example, to be humble, and to consider others before ourselves. Leave the vengeance to God and love in the meantime. It's easier said than done, but the more you seek Him, the more He will reveal to you. Character is built through knowing Him, and your identity is largely determined by that knowledge.

Your identity is more than a name, more than a face. What people say about you is not a reflection of who you are, but what they see. We should be like shining lights in the darkness, but some people don't like the light. They don't want their darkest secrets exposed and don't want to be saved from their sins. That doesn't mean we shouldn't try to lead them to Christ. He alone decides our identity, which may decide the futures of the people in our lives. Identity is not about perspective. It's about truth.

This is why I believe identity plays such a significant role in everyone's lives. I reclaimed my own by finding God. If I would have understood who I was and whose I was while I was going through the pain and agony of being abandoned and hurt, I would not have been in the situation of losing everything. I would not have had the desire to terminate my pregnancy because of a man who no longer desired me or his unborn child.

Although I lost my identity in going through this situation, I knew that it was God's will for me to keep my baby. I somehow realized that I was destined to be my child's mother and it was part of my life journey. I thank God that I did not have the abortion or give my child up for adoption. I birthed an amazing son who is a gift to his family and friends. These circumstances confirmed that only God will continue to be by my side and not leave me.

It was also my belief in God that helped me know that I would experience love again. I was God's child and, although I experienced pain, it was going to be temporary. Lo and behold, I soon met my soul mate, the love of my life, while I was pregnant. God made sure that I met the man who He designed just for me; the man who would love, adore, and honor me as his wife.

If you are currently in a relationship or desire a relationship, make sure you are not looking for that person to validate you. You must always remember that God validated you when He created you. You are the heir, the masterpiece who was fearfully and wonderfully made by Him. You were created in His image, so know and understand your true identity in Christ.

With that being said, it is so important to teach young men and women the importance of their identities. If we know who we are at an earlier age, we can then affirm our identities when we are faced with life challenges. I would be amiss to think that life would be without challenges, but being armed with the knowledge of how to deal with a particular situation could be the deciding factor on how a person may react. Personally, if I did not find God in my situation, I would have gone on a negative life journey. I praise God for helping me get through a painful time that left some residue many years later.

For my sisters: Why would a man ever treat you as a queen, when you don't see yourself as a queen, the masterpiece that God created? Don't dishonor God by playing small or second fiddle to anyone. When you know who you are, you will not settle for a relationship that commands your identity to be validated by a man who does not know who he is. We often settle because we don't value God's creation: Ourselves. We often count ourselves out because we allow the enemy to tell us who we are. We have to position ourselves so that the word of God is a priority in our lives. It is in the word of God that we learn who we are and who God is.

Our earthly status can be shattered in a matter of seconds. Our heads must never get so big that we forget that God created us, as well as heaven and earth. When we lose respect for our Creator and get wrapped up in materialistic things, we lose focus on who God is. I had to be humbled to appreciate that, if I was going to live my life with joy and success, I had to glorify and trust in God. I am nothing without Him.

Have you lost your focus? Has God shown you some painful events? Are you ready to embrace your true identity? Can you look at those painful events and recognize that you wrongly thought that it was all your doing? Know your identity so that you may stop living small. Stand tall on God's word as He and only He knows the plans that He has designed for you.

My Identity Poem

In this weary life, we're called to know just who we are.
When we stand on our Identity, God's grace is never far.
I am a disciple and a follower of Christ.
A mirror of His glory, I reflect His holy light.
Created in his image, it is He who lives in me.
I'm forgiven, for His precious blood has set me free.

When living for eternity, we must know whose we are.
For giving ourselves up to the world leaves an eternal scar.
I belong to Jesus, for I am not of this world.
An heir of God, co-heir with Christ, I'll stand with Christ alone.
I've been transformed by God's great love;
saved from the pit of hell.
When I share in His suffering; His glory's shared as well.

To pursue a life in Jesus Christ, we must know why we're here.
We cannot serve His kingdom until our purpose becomes clear.
I'm here to praise my Savior and give glory to his name.
To make disciples of the lost and let them do the same.
I'm here to know God personally, to love Him with my all.
Through Him I'll do good works and go where He might call.
The 3W life is what I'll live, for I must know my place.
Amazing grace has ransomed me; my sin has been erased.

A Reflection of Me

BONITA PATTON-LOGGINS

"Preserve me, O God; for in Thee do I put my Trust"
—Psalm 16:1

"Without reflection, we go blindly on our way"
—Margaret J. Wheatley

Father, as I open my heart, please guide, guard, and protect me from evil, foreseen and unforeseen, in Jesus Name, Amen. Can you imagine living in a box, poked with holes? That's how I felt for years. Life has been a roller coaster. I've possessed and lost so much but, even after all that I've endured, my relationship and faith in God is stronger. At one time in my life, my tongue was as a corpse cleaved to the roof of my mouth. My presence was invisible and unknown. My voice was silenced. My heart pounded out of rhythm. My mind was overwhelmed, tormented, and disturbed. My shoulders were weighted with burdens. My eyes were strained and tearful, my hands sweaty and shaky, my feet were stagnant and numb. I forced a smile but my screams on the inside were left unheard. I was lost, alone, and afraid to reach or speak out on all I'd endured.

How do you control your tears when they are greater than your fears? What do you do when all you know is a blur? You stand, dry your eyes, pray, and plan.

As the eldest of three children, I played a major role in my home. Mom and Dad worked to provide a comfortable lifestyle and atmosphere for my siblings and me. We lived in areas where our skin tone was very noticeable and observed, and we stood out like a sore thumb. All I knew was to smile, be kind, and show love towards all.

My childhood was fun, but also painful. My father was handsome, humble, loving, strong, an excellent cook and housekeeper like myself, and never met a stranger. Mom worked tirelessly for thirty years. I didn't quite understand why she was so distant and firm, but later in life, I understood how she became the woman she is today. Her own mom passed away from high blood pressure and a broken heart when she was only seven-years-old. I also realized how my father's illness affected her.

Dad would go in and out of diabetic comas. I remember Mom keeping sugar cubes around the house, and she would place one under his tongue as he'd drift off with one eye open. The ambulance was called regularly to our home, since he had many episodes. I stayed in my room most of the time, listening to music—I guess you could say I was a loner. I was expected to keep my grades up, behave appropriately in school, and care for my siblings when my parents were away.

Dad would at times leave and come home sick and fatigued, then suddenly be all right again. One particular time, he instructed us to help him clean the garage out. Dad always made chores fun for us three girls, and afterwards, he cooked a great meal. We had stuffed pork chops and green beans. The meal was heavenly, but something felt weird. The next day, he became ill. The door of my parent's room was open, and when I peeped inside after my mom left for work, I saw him lying in bed with one eye and mouth open the way he often slept. Something told me to stay home with him, but I knew I had to catch the bus, so I left for school. After lunch, my teacher told me to gather my backpack and proceed to the front office. When I arrived, our neighbor from across the street was there to pick us up. Dad was in the hospital.

When we rushed to the hospital, I saw my mom being carried across to another room. I didn't know what was happening. She walked towards my siblings and me with tears in her eyes and told us that our dad had died. I couldn't believe what I had just heard. Our mom took us to see him. He was on a long metal table with a sheet halfway over him with one eye and his mouth open. I didn't shed a tear. My mind went back to before I left for school.

Shortly afterwards, my grandparents came to the hospital, as they always did when my dad had episodes; this time, it was different. I heard my grandmother rush in and ask where my dad was. I heard her shout, "Lord Jesus, not my baby Edward!" My grandfather grabbed his chest and had to be placed on a stretcher.

All I could think of was why I left him home alone. As a twelve-year-old child, this was an enormous pill to swallow.

We went home and everyone came over to the house. I saw my dad's suit on the bed a couple of days later. I thought that he would wake up and come home. But the day of the funeral, I saw him in the casket. I was in shock, but not one tear fell from my eyes. As time passed, I proceeded to take care of the house and my siblings as my mother instructed me to do until I finally realized my dad wasn't coming home again. I blamed myself for my dad's death for thirty-six years.

Many children suffer from various traumatic experiences in life and can't express themselves openly, so don't ignore the cries from within.

After my dad's passing from diabetes in 1981, my life changed in an unfamiliar direction. My mom made the decision to leave our home to move us in with her sister in the projects. Our lives changed drastically. Our family moved from a predominantly Caucasian community to a majority Black complex. I was in total shock by our new environment. Life was rather scary but, eventually, I adjusted. My aunt owned a 1963 Chevrolet Impala, and in the mornings, she took us to school. I soon became curious about the typical pre-teen wonders. I had dreams of boys and sex. Though I would imagine, I dared not proceed to the act due to fear of becoming pregnant, dishonoring Jehovah God, or disobeying my mom, who instilled the fear of God in us at an early age. So, I was obedient and very reserved.

> *"Train up a child in the way that he should go and when he is old he will not depart from it."*
>
> —Proverbs 22:6

We were raised in a Baptist Church but, one day, my mom was approached by Jehovah's Witnesses and she decided to join the Kingdom Hall Fellowship. We attended weekly Sunday service and participated in Bible Study every week at our home. Unfortunately, we never became actual members of the Kingdom Hall but, rather, we became Devout Witnesses. We practiced for years until, one day, a young lady who we studied with became pushy and arrogant towards my mom, so the visits to church halted. My desire was to study Biblical theology and learn of the many different facets of religions, practices, and teachings of Jesus Christ. This continues to be my goal and dream in fulfilling my purpose and calling by God.

Affirmation: I will fulfill this goal, in Jesus Name, Amen.

> *"Death and life are in the power of the tongue; and they that love it shall eat the fruit thereof."*
>
> —Proverbs 18:21 (KJV)

Times became challenging for my mom. She was a single mother at the age of twenty-eight and had suffered a drastic decrease in income. She became depressed and chose alcohol to cope with her hurt and pain. In this season, she met a man at a nearby nightclub and they began courting. Shortly afterwards, we moved to a home on the Southeast side of Fort Worth, in which we resided for a couple of months before she allowed him to move in with us. Not long after this, Mom wed this man.

The enemy comes when we are at our weakest. Remember, not all that shines are diamonds. Take heed when things seem too good to be true. Always research one's background before allowing them into you zone.

As time went along, I attended middle school and worked hard to keep my grades up. One of the most hurtful experiences took place that left my mind at a loss. My mom's lover started to make sexual advances towards me. The first time it happened, everyone was outside. This man was mowing the yard while I swept, since we all pitched in around the house. I was outside in the driveway with a broom in my hand. That was when he told me one of his friends told him that I was fine. I didn't know how to respond and became afraid. I continued to sweep.

My mom had gone into the house to cook, but when she came out, she knew that something was wrong. She then left and went back in the house. I overlooked his comment, seeing that he was intoxicated. But one night, after I bathed, I adorned myself in a beautiful, long gray and white cotton robe my dad had purchased for me from Neiman Marcus years before he passed. I went in the den to play the Atari game system. I sat on the floor, and out of nowhere, my mom's lover came in and lay on the floor. I saw him out of my side view and I couldn't believe what I saw. He only had on his white underwear. I stood up and sat on the couch.

He laid his head on my lap and looked up at me. I didn't know what to do or how to feel, so I pushed him off of me, stood up, and went to my sister's room instead of mine. My mom was asleep, so I didn't go in her room. I feared what he would do. The following morning, I got up to get dressed. I thought everyone had left for work, so I went to use my mom's bathroom and the man walked in. He looked at me in the mirror and began to stroke my hair. He told me how pretty I was. I left in a hurry and was picked up by my best friend to ride to school. That whole day, my head was messed up. The teacher called on me, but I couldn't hear her. My friend asked what was wrong and, though I was hesitant to tell her, I eventually did. She told me to tell my mom to avoid further attempts. She also told her mom after they dropped me off at home.

I walked in the house afraid, but told my mom everything. She became enraged. When her lover arrived, she confronted him. He got in my face, standing tall as to talk over and intimidate me. We moved in with my aunt for a while, but eventually moved back in the house with him, which was devastating. As a child, anger consumed me. I thought, "How could a grown man approach a child this way?" I asked this question daily and was angry with my mom for allowing this to happen, which left my heart hardened towards her into my adult years. Later, he attempted the same thing towards my younger sisters, and the marriage ended in divorce. He never admitted what he did, not even to this day. Still, I had to forgive him, let go, and allow God to handle it.

Forgiveness doesn't excuse the offender's behavior, but prevents them from destroying your heart.

"For if you forgive other people when they sin against you, your Heavenly Father will also forgive you."
—Matthew 6:14

During this experience, I reunited with a young man, who had once briefly pursued me while I was living in the projects. I was twelve and he was fourteen. At the age of fifteen, I became pregnant and my whole life changed. I gave birth to a baby girl. Three years later, I gave birth to another baby girl. The pressure of being a young father took a toll on my boyfriend and his behavior changed. I endured mental and physical abuse. We parted for six months then reunited, and soon after, we wed. Within a year I gave birth to our son. After years of marriage and parenting, my husband's physical and mental health decreased, particularly about six months after I took a job at a known oil and gas company. He became ill and had to be rushed to the hospital. They believed he had cancer but, after all testing, he was diagnosed with a rare disease referred to as Sarcoidosis (a disease that leads to inflammation usually in the lungs, skin or lymph nodes). This prevented him from working any longer; depression and anger came into play and his health further declined.

Our family endured a major financial crisis but we pulled together and trusted God, which got us through.

I enjoyed working at my job, and all was great until, years later, my company was bought out, and I was let go after nineteen years of service. But even after the abuse, the job loss, the nervous breakdowns, the diagnosis of chronic depression, the suicide attempt, and hospitalization in a mental institution, with God, I survived! I found my voice and purpose in life after realizing that it was wrong to desire or attempt to take my life when I didn't create it. Many years, I sat in silence, but one day I had an epiphany and my life flashed before my eyes. I saw my children, my husband, my mother and family standing over my casket, heartbroken and distraught to the point of no return. I owed it first to God, myself, then to family, to take control of my life, mind, and heart. I had to step out on faith by speaking instead of remaining silent, not caring about what others thought or felt about me, and allowing my outside to finally match my inside in a positive way. I found me, Bonita, in the midst of it all. I learned that Bonita is a powerful woman who matters and, no matter if I am alone or surrounded by many, I am still important, valued, and significant. I deserve to love and be loved.

Today, I can honestly say that I am a new person because I trusted God. I allowed myself to feel, breathe, and look in the mirror to love my reflection. I forgave myself for my dad's death, because I learned that things happen in life beyond our control. I forgave my mom's lover by realizing that I would be relinquishing my power, life, thoughts, and behavior over to him if I didn't. After many psychiatric visits, prayer, meditation, Bible study, and reading of God's Word, I learned that, if I didn't forgive, I could never ask God or anyone to forgive me. I had to separate myself from the abuse and the things that weighed me down to regain my identity.

I found my happiness and peace spending time alone at the park, sitting in my car, listening to music and ministry, walking the track, and loving my family and friends. I realized God loves me. I am somebody, I am of worth, and I choose what I accept without regret. I am alive and I didn't die though life tried to destroy and remove me from the earth. I finally gained control of my life and decided to live. The tears I've shed due to pain and hurt are now tears of joy. I now understand that I can't make everyone happy or love me. I learned to love myself despite my past. I am beautiful despite my flaws, and I have purpose that far exceeds what I can imagine. I can do anything that my heart desires and needs. I no longer feel the need to live in the shadows of others and I see my scars as reminders of my past but also testimonies for my present and future. My life belongs to my Creator, Jehovah God who created me and let me belong.

If you are in an unhealthy place or relationship that causes distress, discomfort, or harm, please don't stay. Choose to be free from the bondage that causes you hurt or pain. You don't have to suffer in silence. You don't owe your life to anyone but God and yourself. Reach out to talk to God, and He will reach back to bless and see you through. We must speak life into every dark and non-peaceful place or situation we endure, no matter how it appears or feels. It is crucial to stay focused, positive, and determined to meet any goal we have in life. We can't allow fear of the unknown or current and past circumstances to halt our destiny or dreams already set in place by our Eternal Father in Heaven. We have the power to overcome anything that the enemy uses for evil and turn those things into the inevitable for our own good.

> "But as for you, ye thought evil against me; but God meant it unto good, to bring to pass, as it is this day; to save much people alive."
> — Genesis 50:20 (KJV)

> "But Jesus beheld them, and said unto them, with men this is impossible; but with God all things are possible."
> — Matthew 19:26 (KJV)

16 "YOU" CONVERSATIONS

- You can overcome any challenge or circumstance
- You have control over your life
- You can forgive and be forgiven
- You have power over your adversary
- You can stand tall and be made whole again
- You can achieve all that you hope, wish, and dream for
- You are not your past
- You have a voice
- You have what it takes to make it
- You are the head and not the tail
- You are above and not beneath
- You aren't what your negative thoughts speak

- You don't have to live in fear when you have faith
- You are more than a conqueror
- You are beautiful, loved, smart, and strong
- You belong to the most high God and He loves you

My Identity Prayer

Jesus knew who He was. He knew He was the son of the almighty God! He knew He was the heir of the Kingdom. He knew He was called for a time such as this. Jesus knew His "Why." He knew His purpose. He knew that He would not leave earth until His assignment was fulfilled.

Father, in the name of Jesus, I declare that I am no longer ignorant of Whose I am, who I am, and why I am here. I thank you, Father, for the power that has been revived in me to walk and live within my identity. I am crystal clear of my inheritance and my purpose. I know I was created by You and for You! I thank You Lord that I no longer need to seek validation from a man, because I know now that You validated me when You created me. I thank You, Lord, that I can trust in Your word, which states in Genesis 1:27, that You created me in Your image. I know, Lord, that the power is inside of me to do all things in Christ because You strengthen me. I can walk in boldness because I know that Your word is clear when You said that I was fearfully and wonderfully made.

I thank You, Lord, for what You have deposited in me. My prayer is that my sisters and brothers will come to understand and embrace their true identities so that we can claim our inheritance that is here on earth right here, right now. I declare and decree to embrace my inheritance and to know that I am blessed with every spiritual blessing in Christ as stated in Your word in Ephesians 1:13. Our identity is marked as belonging to You by the Holy Spirit. The Holy Spirit in us is our validation!

I thank You, Lord, for waking me up! I thank You, Lord, for not giving up on me. I thank You, Lord, for never leaving me or forsaking me. I honor and praise You, Lord. You have given us the power and the authority to stamp out demons, heal the sick, pick up our mats, and open up our eyes! I am forever grateful—because You love me, You never left me.

A Reason for Me to Be

TILDA WHITAKER

"Figure out what will please Christ, and then do it."
— Ephesians 5:10 MSG

"How should I do it?" I thought to myself, as I weighed all the options. Even at my worst moments, I am pragmatic. On the darkest night of my life, I wanted to make sure I didn't inconvenience others and make a big mess when I killed myself. I wanted the perfect balance of a painless way to go, a guarantee of success, and the least mess. I was surprised by all the options once I started thinking about it. Thankfully, one of the symptoms of being really depressed is having a hard time making complicated decisions.

God didn't want me to die that night. He had plans for me—a reason for me to be. And that night, He started telling me his plans. I pushed my own plans away and I started listening.

Why am I here? Why is this happening to me? What is my purpose? What is a reason for me to be? These are all questions we ask ourselves usually many times over throughout our lifetimes. Many think they have figured out their purpose without the help of God to direct them—they're just lucky that way. Perhaps, but if God isn't directing things, are they really blessed? Others are happy not operating in their purpose. So far, their life is good; no one is requiring any sacrifices from them and living with the status quo is a desirable thing to them—for now. For most, life is full of peaks and valleys, highs and lows, good times and bad times. And as much as I'd like to tell you it's easy to find a reason to be, most of the time, it's not. It's hard, a struggle. But the end result is a blessing like you've never experienced before.

> "For I know the plans I have for you," declares the LORD, "plans to prosper you and not to harm you, plans to give you hope and a future."
> —Jeremiah 29:11

As much as God loves us and is with us all the time, we hear Him best when we're low, on our knees, crying out in pain and fear, surrendering to the fact that, no matter how hard we're swimming against the current, no real progress can be made without His help.

My moment on my knees, hearing God speak to me about a reason for me to be, came on a dark night in November of 1998. Many find themselves down when their marriage crumbles, their home is in foreclosure, they lose a job, or they're parenting a small child all by themselves. I wasn't struggling with just one of these things, but all of them at once. And I wasn't just "down:" I was deeply depressed, hopeless, humiliated, and in complete despair. The negative voice in my head was telling me that my choices had brought me to this. This was all my fault.

I had played by the rules. I grew up in the church and lived by good principles, by His words. I did what my parents told me to do. I was a good person—so why was this happening to me? The guilt for my life not turning out picture-perfect was buckling down on my shoulders. The shame, the defeat was swallowing me whole. I questioned the very essence of myself, my identity. Who was I? What had happened to me? What was a reason for me to be?

For four months, I holed up at home, removing myself from the outside world, immersing myself in devotions, scriptures, Bible studies, and meditations. I arose in the morning with prayer; I wrote in my journal and prayed in the noonday, and I prayed at night. I was intent on figuring out my purpose in life, the whole time fighting back against the self-doubts and ever-present shame and guilt that threatened my progress. I knew God loved me, but was I worthy? I had lost so much and failed so spectacularly. Sometimes, when you need God the most is when you doubt Him the most.

That November night, the darkness in my head and heart tempted me with its promise of comfort, quiet, and an end to the guilt and shame. Letting the darkness completely swallow me seemed like the most peaceful option. I was weary of swimming upstream and just wanted to stop flailing in waters too deep for me. I wasn't cut out for this river—couldn't I just gently float to the bottom? As I sat in the dark, I wondered: Pills? A gun? How did I want to go?

"And we know that in all things God works for the good of those who love him, who have been called according to his purpose."
—Romans 8:28

That night, on my knees, my answer came. He was near and He spoke to me. It was a voice. I heard it perfectly. Would someone else in the room have heard it? I think so; it was so clear and succinct.

"You can't drown here," He said. "Swim." God told me to swim.

So I started swimming: Toward life, toward the top, toward Him, toward my reason for me to be. As I was swimming out of the darkness, it occurred to me that, as much as I had followed God and Jesus and loved His Word in the past, this time was different. I was of a fifth generation of churchgoers and leaders, but that night was the beginning of the best and most beautiful thing in my life: My personal relationship with God. Before this, I'd always believed in God, but I'd never had a real personal relationship with Him. I love the church I grew up in and will always be thankful for the foundation and love I received there, but really walking with God was opening up a new kind of love for Him. A new kind of faith. And it was beautiful and scary and real and magnificent. He and I were friends; I was his beloved. He didn't care about my past mistakes, bad choices, or weakness in the previous weeks. He loved me. He was going to take care of me unconditionally.

That was the night I found a reason for me to be. The chains of my self-doubt, shame, and guilt sloughed off. I grew stronger, the more I felt Him with me. Cutting through the dark water to the top, I surfaced. My mind cleared. I didn't just hear Him, I felt Him—He embraced me and I embraced Him straight from His word. I was reminded of my devotional read of Ezekiel 47:

¹ The man brought me back to the entrance to the temple, and I saw water coming out from under the threshold of the temple toward the east (for the temple faced east). The water was coming down from under the south side of the temple, south of the altar. ² He then brought me out through the north gate and led me around the outside to the outer gate facing east, and the water was trickling from the south side.

³ As the man went eastward with a measuring line in his hand, he measured off a thousand cubits[a] and then led me through water that was ankle-deep. ⁴ He measured off another thousand cubits and led me through water that was knee-deep. He measured off another thousand and led me through water that was up to the waist. ⁵ He measured off another thousand, but now it was a river that I could not cross, because the water had risen and was deep enough to swim in—a river that no one could cross. ⁶ He asked me, "Son of man, do you see this?"

Then he led me back to the bank of the river. ⁷ When I arrived there, I saw a great number of trees on each side of the river. ⁸ He said to me, "This water flows toward the eastern region and goes down into the Arabah, where it enters the Dead Sea. When it empties into the sea, the salty water there becomes fresh. ⁹ Swarms of living creatures will live wherever the river flows. There will be large numbers of fish, because this water flows there and makes the salt water fresh; so where the river flows everything will live.

My suffering in the dark had not gone unnoticed by God; He had been there all along. As I was swimming to the top, out of the dark depths, I knew my purpose had something to do with helping other women swim out of the bottom of their dark waters. It became clear that I had a voice, mission, and message for other women; after all, I had been there at the darkest dark place, so I knew how to help those who had lost sight of the light. God taught me that, the only way *not* to be afraid of such a place, is to have been there and to know that you can get out. You don't have to drown there.

The idea for a ministry was born that night. The tenants of Single Women In Mission were inspired from the struggles I went through. The genesis of this ministry went from an idea in my head to a full-fledged non-profit organization that serves women searching for their reasons to be, purpose, direction, and help for a better path in life. In just over fifteen years, we have helped over 100,000 women and their families. Through God's direction and help, lives were changed. Single Women In Mission became a guiding light to many women in our community, and also became known by its shortened name: SWIM.

Living out my reason to be me was not an overnight sensation. While obstacles and barriers did seem to miraculously disappear sometimes, there were plenty of hardships and impediments. Most of these barriers occurred in my head. The devil will try to get you to quit. Many times. Thoughts that went through my head included, "You're not good enough to do this," "This will never work," and "Who are you to want to do God's work?"

I found my best defense against these doubts was remaining purposeful about my purpose. I remained clear and resolute about what God was telling me to do. Every step, every prayer, and every moment was intentional, and I was relentless in bringing it back to God. I quickly learned that the times I faltered were when I tried to lead. Prayer, studying God's Word, listening to my faith mentors, and being quiet and listening for God's Word became the center of all that I did. So, as the doubts rolled over me, I just knew what I knew—I let my faith take over and God's hand made changes happen. As important as the ministry and the vision are, the most important part is God's love for me and His hand in guiding me towards His plan. It was never about me but about fulfilling my assigned purpose from God.

Since that dark night, I've never had a moment of doubt about who God is in my life and what He expects from me. Having this vision and acting on it sealed my relationship with Jesus. No matter what happened, where my life took me—up, down, sideways—I knew God had me in His hands. And as my relationship with God took shape over this time, so did SWIM. The mission for the ministry was simple: To help other women struggling in deep waters to SWIM to the other side and find safety and love. To show them the alternative to sinking, and to lead them to shallow waters where they could stand on their own.

SWIM started in Enfield, a tiny town in Eastern North Carolina. For twelve months, it was simply a monthly prayer meeting; in a town with no public transportation or community meeting places, SWIM gathered up women, mostly single mothers living in poverty, who were looking for a way out of some really deep waters. The town let us meet in its Town Hall. Some women traveled an hour to get to the meeting. We prayed, we talked, we cried, and we lifted each other up. We offered a respite in the dark, deep waters.

I started contacting local resource agencies such as social services, churches, employment agencies, and the health department. As I met and got to know the women in the group, I could match them up with resources to help them in their search for a better life for their families. It became a system of meeting, Bible Study, prayer, and case management.

Soon, SWIM grew. We developed relationships with other local non-profits and social service agencies. We began to get referrals and were blessed with volunteers who wanted to help. Donations came in to help with programming and resources. Women I met who were living in poverty went on to become business owners; women who were homeless now *own* homes; women who felt they would never be anything other than unemployed and poor are productive and successfully supporting their families; women with little to no education have gone on to complete college degrees; women with broken marriages are now in restored relationships; and we have seen so many children of these women find a peace and comfort in their families.

SWIM has flourished and was recognized as an important asset on local, state, and national levels, even finding international support and opportunities to share the vision of women helping women. From a dream-vision that came on the darkest of nights, God showed me a way to bring light into the lives of women who are teetering on the brink of giving up. And what I imagined it in my head—it was only a fraction of God's idea. That's what happens when you let God do the work: It's even bigger and better than you could ever imagine. SWIM eventually came to offer transitional housing to women, a free clothes closet for women seeking employment, mentoring relationships with hundreds of women volunteers, a prison ministry, and invitations of multiple national speakers at sold out events throughout various regions.

God guided all that we did. In these tired, hopeless women, we saw Jesus. When you look for God in broken places, you'll find His greatest gifts and feel His love the most. The women we serve, the volunteers, the tired agency employees, all work together to create a giant light-filled circle of love in an area beaten down by poverty and hopelessness. We became His hands. And I found my reason for me to be.

I'm honored I have an opportunity to tell my story in this book, but really, my story is not as important as your story. What is your reason to be?

We are all called on to help others and be mentors to each other. But before we can honestly help someone else know their purpose in life, we have to know ours. You can't lead others when you haven't been there yourself. My night that almost ended in suicide was where I needed to be. I never would have been able to establish SWIM, or later the church plant to save souls for Christ that grew from SWIM, if I hadn't experienced those dark depths.

Let's start figuring you out. What's your story? Here are a few interactive activities to get you thinking, to begin your journey. Be still. Listen for God. Fill in these blanks:

I work with _____ who struggle with _____.
I help them _____ so they can _____.

Answer these questions:
    Who are you?
    Where are you from?
    Why are you here?
    What can you do?
    Where are you going?

One of my favorite ways to get God-centered and look inward is to pray and think about The Serenity Prayer. I challenge you to know how the Serenity Prayer applies to your life. Below is a part of the prayer and some questions for you to answer:

Grant me the Serenity to accept the things I cannot change,
    What is serenity to you?
    What does it look like to you?
    What does it feel like to you?
    What does it mean to accept?
    What, in your life, do you have no control over?
    What are you unable to change?

...the Courage to change the things I can,
What is courage to you?
What does it look like to you?
What does it feel like to you?
How have you demonstrated courage in the past?
What, in your life, do you have control over?
What are you able to change?

...and the Wisdom to know the difference.
What is wisdom to you?
What does it look like to you?
What does it feel like to you?

How do you know the difference between things you can change and things you cannot?

I encourage you to stay connected to the spirit of God daily. Set aside a regular time and place for you to refocus on the reason for you to be. Pray before beginning each day's journey. Make the time to be still, listen, and reflect thoughtfully on what God is speaking to you. This prayer will help you to see that your reason to be will be fulfilled beyond measure.

> Dear Father,
> You have created and assigned a purpose for everything. None of Your words or actions will come back void. I pray to trust You 110% because Romans 8:28 tells me it all works for my good. As Your word tells me in Jeremiah 29:11, You know my plan and purpose, You know my

reason to be. As I seek my reason to be, I am here on purpose for You to do Your Will. My desire is to please You, to follow You, and to do whatever it is that You purposed for me. My mind is open, my heart is willing, and my body is able. I ask You to fill my spirit with Your Holy Spirit so that I may hear and see, do and speak, in accordance to what is pleasing to You. In Jesus mighty name. Amen

Nothing can compete with your God-given Identity. When you realize that God has given you your life and the title of being a co-heir with Christ, there is nothing that can compete with that. At a time when I had given up on myself, it was God who got me through: It was my prayers, it was me knowing that He was going to shine His light on me. I recognized that I was not only worthy, but I had the power inside of me to stand up and stand strong. It was only God, my God, who whispered in my ear that I was His and that I was going to get through this ordeal.

Maybe you are challenged with an experience and need to be reminded of who and whose you are. Maybe you need a reminder that God said, "He would never leave you nor forsake you." I believed God, I trusted God, and I heard God. It was time for me to grow. It was time for me to stop playing small and believe that I was designed to love me for me.

I am both thankful and grateful that God answered my prayers when He allowed me to meet the love of my life, my husband, my hot sauce. God answered my prayers in a big way. If I had not gone through the trial and recognized who I really was by embracing my identity, then I would not have been able to accept the love that was waiting for me.

We have to be intentional about not putting our trust in princes, in whom there is no help. Our help comes only from our Lord and Savior. Go to God. Let our Heavenly Father guide you to his assigned help angels for your life. God is our Soul Source: When our soul connects to Him, He will give us what we need as we navigate through our lives. As the word states "Do not be afraid or discouraged, for the Lord will personally go ahead of you. He will be with you; he will neither fail you nor abandon you" (Deuteronomy 31:8 (NLT)).

Remove You So GOD Can Shine Through

BECKY CARTER

"Be strong and of good courage, fear not, nor be afraid of them: for the Lord thy God, he it is that doth go with thee; he will not fail thee, nor forsake thee."

—Deuteronomy 31:6 KJV

Life has a funny way of getting our attention. I believe we learn lessons from tragedies, failures, and successes. Personally, I try to learn from all situations, negative and positive. I experienced a rough period in my life in which I felt I could not catch a break. I identified that the enemy was attacking me and I did not understand why. During this difficult time, God said that "He would never leave me or forsake me." And while I believed His words, my faith was tested.

Life was good in the Carter household. My husband and I were empty nesters and planning the next phase of our lives. Our retirement goals were our main focus. Both kids were graduated from college, married, and, above all, healthy. Our greatest joy was our granddaughter who we enjoyed visiting and spending as much time with as possible.

We were also finally generating profit from our business and had started to see the fruits of our labor. Professionally, I wanted to excel to another leadership position at my company. I felt blessed to have a job that allowed me to contribute to my household and, though I didn't want to seem ungrateful or unappreciative, I desired more. Deep down inside, I was capable of doing and being more but complacency had gotten the best of me.

My husband and I began our transition from one city to another late in the fall around November. We prayed about our future and what it would look like in the months to come. We put our plan into action and started to execute. Our objective was to maximize our savings, decrease our debt, and limit our spending. We were successful, again, as we had done this before. We downsized and planned to start building our forever-ever home. My sister and brother-in-law blessed our lives by opening up their residence to us while our new place was being built. Their house felt like home because we visited every Sunday after church. By this point, we were well on our way to accomplishing our goals. The limit was beyond the sky as we worked and moved in the right direction. But that was only the calm before the storm.

I had regular weekly meetings with my boss but, one day, I received a thirty-minute meeting request to be held in a conference room downstairs. The subject line was left blank. My spiritual discernment kicked in and I knew there was no way the news would be good. I attempted to dig deeper and ask questions about the meeting but received no real answers. The reply I received was, "I'm not calling the meeting. The powers that be are." My director's response confirmed what I was thinking: This meeting would not be to give me praise for stellar work performance. My heart raced as I headed to conference room, reciting, "No weapon formed against me shall prosper."

But after meeting with three individuals about my not-so-stellar performance, I was devastated. As my husband would say, I felt like I had been beaten with a wet noodle. I was told that my team survey results were some of the lowest in the company, which was alarming. My spirit was officially broken. My leadership experience ranged over fifteen years and I had never been written-up before or had my job threatened. The closing statement on my write-up read, "leading up to and including termination."

I felt unworthy, incapable, devalued, and betrayed. This write-up came from nowhere, and I was angry. My body language was passive aggressive in the meeting. I immediately called my best friend afterwards because our professional roles are similar. She comforted me, lifted me up, said she would be praying for me, and encouraged me to pray as well. My husband was working and couldn't receive calls but, once he came home, I poured my heart out to him. All of my emotions translated over to him. He suggested giving my two-week notice due to unfair treatment. He assured me that I did not have to put up with this nonsense and that he had faith I would find something else. He was being a loving, supportive husband, but my immediate thoughts were: I could never be an educated, stay-at-home, empty nester wife. No way. Not me!

Still perplexed, I wondered what my next steps should be. My support group is small and selective, but I depend on them to hold me accountable. I reached out early one morning to my nephew who is a teacher and minister. He's smart, witty, and faith driven, a true professional who drives thirty miles every day to his dream job. I knew he could shed some light on this situation. I explained to him what happened and he said, "That's complete foolishness." What executive would draw up such documents and counsel their leader in that way? He repeated several times that the executive management team was unprofessional. At the end of our conversation, I felt a bit better because, of course, he was on my side. Another good friend who worked in humans resources for over twenty years shed more light on the situation and helped me understand why I was written up and how to correct my performance. It hurt me to hear some of her suggestions and rationale but, deep down, I knew she was only trying to help.

I attempted to move on but could not get passed how I was being treated. Reporting to work every day was a struggle. The weekly meetings seemed like whippings and had me at my wits end. My emotions about the entire situation were mixed because my character was being torn to shreds. Personal character is a huge leadership quality, and I would rather be beaten than to have my character tarnished. The constant negative feedback was so specific and personal that it became unbearable to hear. I could not believe the things people said about me, especially when I knew which individuals said what. I was told that I wasn't present, I didn't give positive feedback, I showed no expression, and sometimes, could be perceived as negative. The list went on and on. A few folks said that I ate lunch and put makeup on at my desk and how that was unprofessional, even though everyone at the company ate meals at their desks because the culture we promoted was laid back. Even after I received this feedback, I was expected to be engaged with my employees and do it with a smile on my face.

My work emails were dissected on a daily basis. Each grammatical error, incomplete thought, or incorrect piece of information was sent back to me highlighted in yellow for correction. It got to the point where I had someone proofread my emails before I sent them out. I didn't want any back and forth communication of what I did wrong. I was also given a long list of items I needed to complete to "fix myself," which included books focusing on attitude adjustment, trust, compassion, and self-awareness. Each week, I had to meet with the executive leadership team and report what I had done to make improvements in those areas. There even was a tick sheet used to track my weekly progress.

My every move was monitored and I felt I couldn't do anything right. My bathroom prayer sessions become more intense and frequent. These sessions were an extension of my morning prayer and scripture time, and I couldn't make it through the day without them. I placed encouraging post-it notes on my desk and my coffee cup read "God gives His hardest battles to His strongest soldiers." This cup accompanied me into my weekly meetings with my director and his boss—it was my armor when I went to battle and I made sure the words were turned towards the management team. The scripture that hung in my cubicle read, "Work willingly at whatever you do as though you were working for the Lord rather than people." This scripture gave me strength and hope, and it continued to help me understand that some situations are bigger than me, and God will work it out.

The weekly meetings continued for over a month. My emails continued to be a topic of discussion and were brought to my attention on a regular basis. There was no positive feedback and no plan that included tips for success. My passive aggressive behavior was on display and the executive team could see I was uncomfortable and afraid. The next major meeting I attended was with Director of HR. I took a skill test a few weeks prior to the meeting to test my strengths and weaknesses in my role. This test seemed unnecessary since I had been with the company for over six years and had never been tested on my skills. In my heart of hearts, I knew it was one more strike that could be used to terminate my employment.

The results of the skills test were not good and fell in line with the horrible survey results I received. The feedback focused on all my weaknesses once again and a small percentage of my strengths—heartbreaking! That was my final straw. I knew the end of my employment was near. I loved my peers and had met great folks along the way but it was not enough to make me stay. The job search began, and I needed to know if I was still employable. I stepped out on faith and uploaded my resume to several employment sites. It was scary because the job market had changed but I was determined to leave my company. I was done!

My stress levels were at an all-time high and I was extra worried, especially because I had a few family members with serious health issues. My father-in-law was admitted to the hospital at the tender age of ninety-seven, and he had lost a large amount of blood and needed a blood transfusion; he had also been losing weight at a rapid pace for months.

In addition, I had two very sick nieces, one with cancer and one who needed a kidney transplant, and they were fighting for their lives. In honesty, my focus should not have been on work drama, but on my family. Then, as if I needed anymore trouble at work, my social security number was stolen from the work database. There was no way this was happening to me. My husband and I were purchasing a home and my credit report needed to reflect positive activity. This was not the time for my social security number to be compromised. Life was getting the best of me.

I eventually received several calls from recruiters wanting to set up job interviews; finally, it seemed as if there was some light at the end of the tunnel. My cell phone usage was prohibited at work (one of the things I needed to eliminate or limit due to perception), which made the job search challenging. My team failed to realize I read my work email using the company cell phone and it could be used on the floor. I had to step away from my desk to return calls, emails, and text messages. A well-known company based in several cities throughout the States scheduled me for an interview.

The interview went well and I was immediately scheduled for a second interview. I was super excited! My confidence level shot through the roof, especially when the company called me back and offered me the job. The position was identical to my current position but the salary was lower; still, I was willing to accept a lower paying job just to get out of the situation I was in. However, the very next phone call I received from my loan officer floored me. I discussed the new job with her and she said, "Absolutely not. If you take a lower paying job, you will not qualify for the house." Once again, I was crushed. My chance to move forward was taken away. I immediately started to pray and ask God to reveal to me what was going on. I asked Him to send me signs and show me myself.

The next week, my father-in-law was admitted back into the hospital, this time for pneumonia. The doctors told us he was very sick because of his age and that he could not leave the hospital until the infection in his lungs cleared up. The prognosis was not good but the family stayed in prayer and gave it all to God. He was on a breathing ventilator for over twenty-four hours, and the doctors explained that the period after the ventilator was removed would be crucial. If he breathed on his own, he had a chance. Pops, as I called him, said he asked God for one hundred years and he believed he was going to make it.

One evening, my husband called and said, "Pops is up talking. He's slow and weak but his memory is sharp and clear." I was so thankful to God for his recovery. The very next day, I went to sit with him at the hospital until my husband arrived. He couldn't eat solid food but was given liquids. His throat was sore from the ventilator so I had to swab his mouth with water to keep him hydrated. Though he struggled to sit up, so frail and weak, he never once complained about being in pain. He treated the medical staff with the utmost respect. Every time I gave him water and scratched his back, he said, "Thank you, daughter-in-law."

In the face of his illness, he remained humble and thankful. I sat there and stared at him, deeply in awe of his determination, even when the doctors said they were surprised he had made it. His will to live was unwavering and he was willing to stay the course with humility and grace. After I left the hospital, my mentality started to change. I spoke to God and said, "Thank you for showing me myself."

The struggle at work continued but I pushed through. The emails correcting my work became more frequent and intense than ever. I was so stressed about being right that all my tireless efforts seemed to be wrong. The most degrading responsibility I had was sending out a monthly calendar that let my teams know where I would be during the day. The calendar included my arrival and departure times, weekly scheduled meetings, and my lunchtime. The calendar had all planned vacation and paid holidays as well. Any time I had a reoccurring meeting, an update to the calendar was resent to my team.

The micro management style of the executive leadership team really got under my skin. My assistant VP was responsible for giving my manager my "weekly orders," which, I could tell, made my manager very uncomfortable. His dialogue with me sounded as if he had been coached on what to say regarding my performance: I was unprofessional in communicating with my team, my calculations of their performance were incorrect, I used too many decimal points on the percentages I sent out on weekly sales reports. On top of that, I had a plethora of reports that had to be emailed weekly. Before sending each report, I had to email my team and let them know what time they would receive their reports and, if I could not meet that deadline, I had to send another email to let them know the report would be late. At this point, I believed I would have been better off being fired or taking the lower paying management job.

I prayed and prayed. I said, "Lord, something has to give. I'm at my breaking point." My cousin, who I talked to every other day, gave it to me straight. He simply asked me, "Can you achieve all the things they are asking of you?" I said, "Yes." He told me to get my attitude in check and do more everyday than what was expected. He said my performance needed to be excellent and, if I had been slacking on the job, I was wrong.

He said, "Never take your job for granted. It's a blessing. You are a child of God and this is what He expects of us. You must do what is right as long as you are with the company." He ended the conversation saying, "You can't go to a new job doing the same old things you are doing at your existing one. You have to change, Boo."

God showed me what the problem was and confirmed it through others. It was loud and clear: I was the problem. I was a leader and expected my team to follow my lead but they had lost trust in my leadership. My job was to be an influence, someone who gave them the tools to be better, but my attitude needed adjusting. My level of compassion and understanding needed work. I had done a lot of things wrong and was standing in my own way. God was trying to teach me to seek him first in everything I do, and to not just say it, but to put it into action. Once I decided to hold myself accountable, things started to change for the better.

A follow-up focus group was held with my team two months into my action plan. While there were areas that needed continued improvement, the overall review was good. The feedback was positive and the team could see a real effort in me to improve morale and be supportive.

True growth can only come through change. I had to be willing to be wrong and confess that I messed up in a lot of areas. My performance numbers were consistently above the company goal for more than six years, but the real lesson was about how I treated others. God showed me that I had to love the unlovable, love those who slander my name, and be compassionate to those who need compassion. Above all, I must pray for everyone I work with as if I am praying for my own family and friends. After all, God is Love.

Reflections:

1. As Christians, we are to put God first in all that we do (Matthew 6:33).
2. Finish strong: Don't give up. See your mission, your goal, and your plan through to the end (Ecclesiastes 9:11).
3. Operate out of excellence: Don't half step. Your ultimate boss is God (Colossians 3:23).
4. Trust God in all situations: Believe that He will deliver (Proverbs 3:5).
5. Do what is right (Galatians 6:9).
6. Love your enemies (Matthew 5:44).
7. Worship while you wait: Have faith that He will answer your prayers (Hebrews 11:1)

In My Sight

TABITHA WRIGHT-POLOTE

"Teach me, O Lord, the way of thy statues; and I shall keep it unto the end. Give me understanding and I shall keep thy law; yea, I shall observe it with my whole heart."

—Psalm 119

"Yea though I walk through the valley of the shadow of death, I will fear no evil: for thou art with me; thy rod and thy staff they protect me. Thou preparest a table before me in the presence of mine enemies: thou anointest my head with oil; my cup runneth over. Surely goodness and mercy shall follow me all the days of my life: and I will dwell in the house of the Lord forever."

—Psalm 23

I carry the burdens, weight, and pain of my family's hurt, and I don't know how to let it go. I'm there for everyone all the time but, when I need help or a pick-me-up, where is my rock? I feel like I have to stand on a slippery slope all alone. Constantly, my feet try to stay planted but my mind is scared and my heart is broken into a million pieces. It must end. I must end it with the help of the Lord and the knowledge of discernment.

My time is limited and I do not know which way to turn, for this world has chewed me up. The enemy is running amuck and it seems I have no luck. Help me, Lord, I cry out to Your name. I'm a soldier on the battlefield and my uniform is full of blood. Help my flesh to understand me for I do not understand myself. A child of Yours, created in Your image, developed in utero a child of innocence, born to a world of pure violence. Teach me how to transform these words into wisdom to uplift me. Help me, oh Lord, for I can't keep up this fight. I'm tired and weary and my flesh is full of spite.

Sometimes, I wonder what God's plans are for me because I go through so much. I ask myself, "God, are you pleased with me?" I turn to my faith to keep working and striving to be a better servant for the Lord. Though I am still flesh and I error, I realize that having faith is what keeps me going when I feel stepped on and over. The hurt and disappointment doesn't disappear and I carry this pain for months, sometimes years. But, with God, all things are possible and I am satisfied. My spirit may feel dead, but the faith I have is greater than all the land and stronger than a mustard seed. In my mind, I tried to stop the trauma from playing over and over again but it just wouldn't stop. I felt like I was going crazy within my own body and, the louder I screamed for someone to help and hear me, the worse it got. The softer I whispered my pains, the more they fell on deaf ears. The hurtful part was that they were the ears of the ones I loved so much, those who I was always there for with a smile on my face and a pep in my step, who told me that they loved me too. What I needed was a hug and someone to visit and shower me with love while I was processing everything in my life. I really needed their support.

But I didn't let the lack of care for me defeat me. I didn't allow them to change me into someone I wasn't. God gave me a loving, caring, humble, and giving heart with no strings attached. However, I am flesh and I have pains and feelings and tears. Through too many tears and sleepless nights, I have carried issues that were not mine to bear. I prayed to give them to the Lord but the weakness of my flesh kept picking them up. The cycle proved to me that I needed to grow stronger in Christ to handle issues with faith, not flesh.

> "Teach me that I may walk worthy of the Lord unto all pleasing, being fruitful in every good work, and increasing in knowledge of God; strengthen with all might, according to his glorious power, unto all patience and longsuffering with joyfulness; giving thanks unto the Father, which hath made us meet to be partakers of the inheritance of the saints in light."
>
> —Colossians 1:10-11

When in all God's creation would all this rage and pain stop? All the hurts, pains, angst, frustrations, vigor, violence, cursing, fighting, demanding, failing, and contemplation to end it all. I wondered, "Maybe if I blow my head off, someone will listen." But that would be cheating myself out of a rich life and what God has planned for me. I am created perfect in His image: Ecclesiastes 7:17 says, "Be not overmuch wicked, neither be thou foolish: why should thou die before thy time?" How dare I steal this story of my life?

As far back as I can remember, I always waited for my father to come pick me up. Sitting in the window, pulling at my mom's clothes, running to the next window especially on those hot summer days when the curtain sheers blew all over the house, I just knew he was coming. I knew, any second, I was going to hear the roar of the GTO engine coming up that street so that he could pick me up. I could hang my hand out the car window and fight the wind because I knew my little hand was stronger and that I was stronger and that was final.

I never stopped waiting and I never stopped loving my father. I wanted my father to love me like daddy's little girl in every sense of the word but, after the war, he was hooked on drugs like so many other veterans of World War II. I never knew it until I was in my late teens. I never saw my dad messy, incoherent, or out of sorts in my sight: He was my hero and he still is in my sight. I love my daddy. He worked hard all his life and retired after twenty-seven years of being at the local plant. I still look out the window when I'm at my mother's home, waiting for him to come get his baby girl to take her for that ride, to feel the wind in my hand. I still get butterflies when I see him. I will always honor my mother and father for my days will be longer upon this land which the Lord my God giveth me (Exodus 20:12).

Still, Daddy left an empty hole in my heart for forty-four years, but I thank God everyday for every chance I have to talk to him, hug him, love him, share stories with him, and forgive him for past hurts and future disappointments. We both understand that we love each other and that is all that matters. I've needed that love and support. I needed his encouragement when I started to date and when I became a wife. I wanted him to hold me and tell me how much he loved me and how cruel this world could be. I needed my daddy but daddy needed himself first.

My father gave life to four children outside of my mother, I have been the epitome of a big sister. I mean, all-in with both feet, with the full support of my husband of twenty years. Never did I say "No" to an idiotic idea or circumstance or dumb reason to help a sibling. It was as simple as "Yes." They are my siblings and it's the right thing to do. My baby sister, KD, knows she's hurt me the most. From the time that I was about seven, our relationship was difficult. We had different mothers, and I didn't have a close bond with KD because I wasn't taught to. I do remember she always had a Christmas gift for me and I never had any for her and that made me feel sad. I made a vow that, when I got old enough and had my own money, I'd make Christmas different for her and I. Until then, I made anything my creativity would allow: A fancy card, a crafty pin, a pretty barrette. Once, I was even able to buy her some clothes.

Then, we grew up. KD lost her mother to a horrible disease, and she became a part of the trap life. Cops were always at her house, week after week. She was fighting with this girl, that boy, arguing, falling out with her children's father, going to jail. All the while, I was eight hundred miles away, getting these telephone calls that hurt my soul. Once again, I'd have to tell my husband, "I need to fly home. My sister is in trouble and I need to go lay eyes on her and make sure she's okay." He'd reply, "Whatever you need, my love."

I once witnessed cops pulling KD out her home, assault rifles and 9mm glocks surrounding her, and I heard all kinds of disparaging comments about her home and how she was living. I argued with the officers, bold like Samson facing Goliath without fear, because, though I walk in the valley of the shadow of death, I will fear no evil for God is with me (Psalms 23). Thanks to the NAACP, I acted as her personal liaison until her attorney could arrive.

"Where is your search warrant?" I asked. "Where is your commanding officer? Where is your lead investigator? Why are you violating her civil rights? Why are you pointing that loaded firearm at a cuffed, cooperating suspect? Is her name on the warrant? Where is the warrant? I demand to see it now. My momma didn't raise no dummy and I didn't go to college to be one. Now, show me the paper and get clothes on KD before you're on the news."

Next thing you know, I'm in the interrogation room. Yes, they took her to the station and booked her. The detectives tried to pick me for information, but the only problem was, I had none to give. I hadn't had any time to talk to KD. The only thing that kept running through my head was first 48. I prayed to God to keep my sister safe. I know she was scared out her mind.

No thank you on the water, no thank you on coffee, no need to run my prints, I have no criminal history past or present. No, I do not know why you are holding her or why you entered her home. I requested the warrant and was refused it at her home and the officers made many racially disrespectful remarks that I personally heard. How were we going to handle that?

The detective was so dumbfounded that he just asked me to call him if I came up with any information. My sister ending up being locked up for almost thirty days and. when she came out, she brought the same stinking thinking attitude with her. Sometimes we learn and sometimes we don't.

I also have a baby brother named Zelly. Now, we have a street bond. You know the kind: You see him in the streets and you hug each other, rap a few words, and he promises to call you but never does. One night, he decided to take some street drugs called "WET," which is a cigarette dipped with formaldehyde, and he jumped through a glass window. He was sent to the trauma center of Lehigh Valley Hospital, and again, I got that phone call eight hundred miles away. I was told he coded twice and they didn't know if he was going to make it. I was sick to my stomach, shaking and crying. My husband just held me tight and let me weep into his strong arms until I was able to compose myself back to reality. He said again, "Whatever you need, my love. You must go. This is family." Just like that, I was off

On my flight, I had time to prepare my mind and rationalize what I was going to see. I prepared my eyes to see tubes coming from his body and him barely being able to talk or move. I thought he would be sedated and sleeping with family standing by his bedside, crying in disbelief. "Why would he do something so stupid?" they would be asking themselves. "How long would his recovery time be?"

But when I arrived, the situation was nothing like that. There were no family members or friends there. He was alone. When I walked into his hospital room, Zelly had urinated on the floor. When I asked him why he had done that, he said, "I'm ready to get the fuck out of here." Really? Are you kidding me? I rushed to him, thinking he was almost dead, and now he was being disrespectful? Pitiful. The way I understand, he still lives like he forgets to give God thanks. He doesn't understand that he came through that code blue on his life because of God's grace. Man called a code blue but God called Code Technical on the play and said, "No, not your time son," and breathed life back into his body.

No matter what my siblings have done to me and what they haven't done for me, God kept my heart pure. He taught me to continue to do what is right, no matter how my flesh may feel. The scale was tilted in the most unbalanced of ways, but God is fixing this pain I feel inside. I will keep praying, I will keep smiling, and I will not give up. Lord, keep me close to You, guarded under Your garment. I am weak and I need You.

You can go to church every Sunday but you only get what is being preached when you allow God's light to start shining through you and in you. Let God's mercy overtake your life and soul and begin working in you. He has to—He promised. That is why it's so easy for me to forgive and apologize. I fault often and I'm not perfect but to say sorry and mean it is the only way I can stop theses traumas in my head. Forgive to release your burden.

We often speak hurtful words that are like lashes of the whips on our ancestor's backs. We don't realize we are hurt and hurting; only after seeing the truth about ourselves can we acknowledge our wrongs. Finish hurting if you must, curse if you must, but you must become silent and let God in right at that moment. Cry, hug, apologize, and begin the healing process the best you know how. That's called God's grace.

I'm thankful for God's grace. One day at work, I had a serious allergic reaction to paint that caused me to stop breathing and I died right there in the nurse's office. I had the most beautiful experience with God. It was not a bright light, more like a hue of warm white, a feeling that I just can't describe. It was a place of complete peace and total silence. I could not tell you if it was a man's voice or a woman's voice but I was told, "Not your time." But I didn't want to leave that place; I wanted to stay forever and be warm and at peace.

"I have a plan and a purpose," I was told. God knew that my work and will were for the greater good but I was too busy holding it in, running from the assignment He ordered for me. I knew it but had yet to surrender to His calling. If I didn't unveil my talents, God was going to remove them from my life forever.

My second experience with death happened when I had five pulmonary embolisms in my left lung and two in my arm. God spoke to me in a dream that I was going to die. The next day, I had a scheduled appointment with my pulmonologist and I told him about my dream. He didn't believe me at first, but I challenged him and, truth to the Almighty, they found the blood clots. I ended up spending ten days in the hospital and my KD came to see me one time (Zelly didn't come see me at all). My dad came to see me and laughed and joked with me but my praying saint, my mom, came almost every day. I thank God for her.

My mother is tough on me in many ways and sometimes she hurts my feelings with her words and actions, but she always says they will make me stronger. I agree with her some days but, on many of those days, I just need a hug. I'm fighting enough demons and I don't always need a lesson; sometimes, I just need love and affection.

But my mom is the sounding board for everyone, always listening to problems and issues. It's what makes her strong and a leader. I often think, "Who is her sounding board?" That's why I believe that therapy was one of the best forms of help I could have ever sought and received. It was a safe place where I was able to learn to listen and listen to learn, which is the key to overcoming everything in life.

We can't always expect the greatest results to come out of the turmoil in our lives, but we can always hope, at some point, to forgive and eventually forget. I have been through traumas that have left me empty and broken hearted but I will never give up on the possibility of unity and compassion. At times, I have been broke without a penny to my name but God has always provided when the time was right and sheltered me through the storms. He surrounded me with a garrison of angels when my spirit was broken and I didn't know which way to turn.

It's okay to be broken, battered, bruised, and lost, so long as you keep on pressing. When you decide to stop trying is when you fail and the devil wins with all the victories. We walk by faith, not by sight, and when we pray for one another every day for one minute, we have made a covenant with God to be each other's keepers. That is called love, the only thing God will judge us by in the end.

Major Depressive Disorder: It's a Journey, Not a Destination

VENESSA D. ABRAM

"I waited patiently for the LORD; he inclined to me and heard my cry. He drew me up from the pit of destruction, out of the miry bog, and set my feet upon a rock, making my steps secure. He put a new song in my mouth, a song of praise to our God. Many will see and fear, and put their trust in the LORD."

— Psalms 40:1-3

My name is Venessa D. Abram, a Gary, Indiana native who was relocated by my employer to Atlanta, Georgia four years ago. I am married to my loving husband of twenty-two years and we are blessed with three precious adult children and a thirteen-year-old cocker spaniel. I love the Lord and was baptized at age seventeen. As delightful as this all sounds, I struggled with bouts of depression that affected every area of my life.

There were times throughout my adult life that I encountered extreme sadness and hopelessness and I could not understand why my emotions were in disarray. It was a constant battle until my life became unmanageable and uncontrollable. It was in my thirties when I sought medical attention and was diagnosed with depression.

Major depressive disorder (MDD), is a mental disorder characterized by at least two weeks of low mood that is present across most situations. It is coupled by low self-esteem, loss of interest in normally enjoyable activities, low energy, and pain without a clear cause. MDD can also be connected with suicidal thoughts.

Prior to seeking medical attention, my days would begin with dire sadness and feelings of unworthiness, helplessness, hopelessness, no appetite, and exhaustion at every waking moment of my days. This continued until my life spiraled out of control and I could no longer tolerate nor fight the feelings and emotions that were raging. I was unable to function and perform my job requirements with excellence as I typically do, or live my home life.

My depression was offset by life events that were outside of my control. The deaths of my mother and brother were the most difficult times in my life. As a Christian and a believer in Jesus Christ, I understand that there is eternal life after death. Nevertheless, in my humanity, I was broken, hurt, confused, angry, lost, hopeless, and in deep despair. John 11:23-26 states:

> *Jesus said to her, "Your brother will rise again." Martha said to him, "I know that he will rise again in the resurrection on the last day." Jesus said to her, "I am the resurrection and the life. Whoever believes in me, though he die, yet shall he live, and everyone who lives and believes in me shall never die. Do you believe this?"*

As I entered my grief journey, depression began to set in and I spiraled downward mentally, emotionally, and spiritually. After several months of being unable to move forward, I sought professional help from a doctor who diagnosed me with MDD and started me on a regimen of medication, psychotherapy, and grief counseling to start me on the road recovery. Although I was not fond of taking depression medication, I was desperate to feel better and come out of my dark space, so I promised myself I would take all medicines prescribed to me for as long as the doctor told me to stay on them. My appointments were scheduled every two weeks during which I would speak with my therapist and begin the journey of healing from grief.

But due to the stigma that comes with depression, I was afraid of being judged by others for my shortcomings. I was so afraid that I tried to hide the fact that I was taking medicine from my husband and family until I could no longer cover up the truth about depression. I had to face myself and come to terms with the fact that I may need stay medicine-compliant possibly for the rest of my life. I was tired of merely existing and I wanted to live with meaning and purpose, so I began to pray fervently, asking God to help me: "Lord, thank You for this day. There has to a better way of life than how I am living. You did not create me to live a life of emotional and mental instability but one full of potential and purpose. Father, create in me a clean heart and renew a right spirit within me so I may live in unison with You and in Your will. Amen."

As I reflect back, my struggles started when I inadvertently played the role of "be all" to everything and everybody around me, which is mentally draining to say the least. I am the type of person who works toward excellence, and I have passion for people. But I learned very quickly that people were taking advantage of my kindness and had ulterior motives. It was then that I became mentally and emotionally stressed and noticed my body responding with migraines, anxiety, and body aches and pains that were later diagnosed as fibromyalgia.

Fibromyalgia is a disorder categorized by widespread musculoskeletal pain accompanied by fatigue, sleep, memory, and mood issues. Researchers believe that fibromyalgia amplifies painful sensations by affecting the way your brain processes pain signals. Symptoms sometimes begin after a physical trauma, surgery, infection, or significant psychological stress. In other cases, symptoms gradually accumulate over time with no single triggering event. Women are more likely to develop fibromyalgia than men, and those who have fibromyalgia have irritable bowel syndrome (IBS), tension headaches, temporomandibular joint (TMJ) disorders, anxiety, and depression. There is no cure for fibromyalgia, but a variety of medications can help control symptoms along with exercising, relaxing, and stress-reduction measures to reduce episodes.

My rheumatologist prescribed me Lyrica, which treats both depression and fibromyalgia, along with some physical therapy twice a week to aide in the relief of my muscle aches and pain. It finally hit me like a ton a bricks. I realized that I was taking on responsibility and burdens of others that were not mine to carry to begin with. I was at the end of myself and needed to surrender to God. I was afraid of the unknown future, but I was more afraid of staying the same or becoming worse, so I took my leap of faith and put my trust in God.

As I meditated daily and spent quality time with God, my perspective on life changed. God explained in great detail that I am not built to carry burdens: "Come to me, all who are weary and burdened, and I will give you rest" (Matthew 11:28). The more I was in the presence of God and His word, the more I became spiritually filled and empowered by the Holy Spirit. And it is important to note that, while a relationship with Christ is absolutely necessary, I was responsible for being medicine compliant and making sure I attended my physical therapy sessions in order to heal and get better.

Statistics reveal that 350 million people suffer from depression, but many do not seek the help they need, resulting in dire consequences that can lead up to suicide. The stigma that is placed on having depression oftentimes can make it difficult for someone to seek medical treatment and begin the road to healing, health, and stability. Although there are various types of depression, it is highly recommended for one to seek professional treatment when feeling hopeless and depressed.

The journey of depression is a never-ending road and has its ebbs and flows, just as any illness does. However, I learned about the illness, my triggers, and their effects, which helped manage my symptoms. I discovered I was placing too much pressure on myself to work as a perfectionist, both at home and on the job. My perfectionist attitude included working until all the work was done; taking on too much responsibility without delegating tasks to others; being overworked and not appreciated and valued; and being a daughter, wife, mother, sister, student, and employee all simultaneously. Having this type of high-stress lifestyle coupled with life events became unbearable and I broke.

I made the decision to try a new way of living by learning coping skills and strategies that would lessen stress and control both my depression and fibromyalgia. Coping skills are systems and methods put in place to utilize during high stress moments. The more I practiced the skills, the more they became habits, and I was mindful of how they worked when I exercised them. One of my most effective coping skills is to create healthy boundaries: Having boundaries with myself and others allows me to check in on my priorities and stay focused by not compromising my integrity, morals, and values for others. I also exercise mindfulness, a mental state achieved by focusing one's consciousness on the present moment, while calmly recognizing and accepting all feelings, thoughts, and bodily sensations. And lastly, I constantly remind myself I can only change myself and not people, places, or things around me. I pray this prayer quite often:

> "God grant me the serenity to accept the things, I cannot change; courage to change the things I can; and wisdom to know the difference. Living one day at a time; enjoying one moment at a time; accepting hardships as the pathway to peace; taking, as He did, this sinful world as it is, not as I would have it; trusting that He will make all things right if I surrender to His Will; that I may be reasonably happy in this life and supremely happy with Him forever in the next. Amen."

Now, doing the recovery work from depression is very intense, emotional, complicated, and quite difficult to say the least. However, all the time, blood, sweat, tears, and unpacking emotional baggage has been well worth it. We will encounter troubles in this life, but please remember that we are not built to carry the burdens of this world. We are to give them to our Heavenly Father and to use our God-given common sense to seek professional help in whatever capacity necessary for betterment of one's health. Never be embarrassed to seek therapy in one form or another or to take medications for long periods of time or maybe even for the rest of your life. The important thing is that you can live abundantly and full of God's light and purpose: "The thief comes only in order to steal and kill and destroy. I came that they may have and enjoy life, and have it in abundance [to the full, till it overflows]" (John 10:10).

When I yearned to have a closer relationship with God and spent time praying, reading the Bible, and worshipping God on a daily basis, I noticed a supernatural shift. I noticed my depression was lifting and God was in His rightful place in my life and soul, which resulted in my receiving the Lord's love, peace, joy, grace, mercy, wisdom, courage, understanding, revelation, knowledge, and strength for my journey. I learned that, in my own strength, I can do nothing, but in the Lord's strength, I could do all but fail. We can only do so much as humans, and when we force something that should not be, we become dismantled from the seats of our souls. This leaves an open door for depression or other illnesses to come into your life, and without proper care and professional attention, those distractions will delay you to your destiny.

Although I was in pain during these seasons in my life, I realize there is truly purpose in pain. God does His best work when we are in the dark or in the midst of our valleys. He showed me that everything in life has His perfect design and divine timing that will result in his promises being fulfilled.

Ecclesiastes 3: Everything Has Its Time

To everything there is a season,
A time for every purpose under heaven:
A time to be born, and a time to die;
A time to plant, and a time to pluck what is planted;
A time to kill, and a time to heal;
A time to break down, and a time to build up;
A time to weep, and a time to laugh;
A time to mourn, and a time to dance;
A time to cast away stones, and a time to gather stones;
A time to embrace, and a time to refrain from embracing;
A time to gain, and a time to lose;
A time to keep, and a time to throw away;
A time to tear, and a time to sew;
A time to keep silence, and a time to speak;
A time to love, and a time to hate;
A time of war, and a time of peace.

Many people suffer in silence when it comes to depression; that's why depression is known as the "Silent Killer." People with depression fight a battle every single day of their lives. Many people in society, even those in high stature and the public's eye, have succumbed to suicide due to their depression and mental challenges. Suicide is a tragic, painful, and traumatic experience that is the worst-case scenario for someone struggling with depression. Frequent thoughts of suicide, or hurting oneself or others are common symptoms of depression. Should you have such thoughts, please don't wait until it's too late. Ask for help. Depression can't be "cured," but can be treated by a medical professional. Depression varies from person to person and does not go away overnight. Therefore, if someone makes comments for you to "get over it or suck it up," don't take that advice.

Several ways to treat depression include psychological counseling, medication, hospitalization, and even exercise. Medication helps improve symptoms and allows you to return to the things that bring you joy in life. Taking medication is not a sign of weakness but a sign that one is on the road to recovery, health, and holistic healing.

Major Depressive Disorder (MDD) is not a destination, but a lifelong journey that I must hold myself accountable to and take all measures necessary against so I can live my life with passion for my purpose, which means putting my health first. Please understand that you are not alone if you are suffering in silence or have been diagnosed with depression. My suggestion is for you to seek the medical attention necessary, while complying with medications and therapy sessions so your life can become balanced and healed in the direction of peace and prosperity. Here are just a few types of depression listed below:

- Major Depression
- Persistent Depressive Disorder.

- Bipolar Disorder
- Seasonal Affective Disorder (SAD)
- Psychotic Depression
- Peripartum (Postpartum) Depression
- Premenstrual Dysphoric Disorder (PMDD)
- Situational Depression

If you think you suffer from any of these, please seek medical attention immediately. Should you ever feel suicidal or homicidal, please call 911 so that an emergency personnel can be dispatched to your location. Below you find more resources:

National Suicide Hotline: 1-800-273-TALK (8255)
Veterans Crisis Line: 1-800-273-8255 (Press 1)
https://www.veteranscrisisline.net/
https://suicidepreventionlifeline.org/
http://www.suicide.org/suicide-hotlines.html

Through my self-discovery journey with depression, God has blessed me immensely with His divine love, wisdom, knowledge, revelation, courage, direction, and strong support system. A system can be made up of your family, friends, church family, etc. Having this system makes the journey not as complicated and lonely, and can provide you with a net of love, care, and concern that helps the healing process even more. When you are in a crisis, make sure you are able to speak soundly or have a designated person who will speak on behalf of your medical care and treatment. Doing this will allow you to receive the necessary treatment that is most beneficial to your specific condition or diagnoses. If this is not in place, you may run the risk of not receiving the critical and specific care needed for total healing and restoration during your time of need.

Never be ashamed of depression. Be strong and courageous and fight moment to moment for God's purpose in your life: "The Lord himself goes before you and will be with you; he will never leave you nor forsake you. Do not be afraid; do not be discouraged" (Deuteronomy 31:8).

Venessa's Prayer for Depression

Father God, thank You for Your unwavering love and never-ending grace and mercy that keeps us moment to moment, day to day. I pray, Dear God, that You will touch each person that is dealing with depression, and mental and emotional suffering. I declare You will give them peace that surpasses all understanding and let them know that You are the great "I Am," and that You will never leave or forsake them.

Father, I pray that no weapon formed against them shall prosper and You will build a strong hedge of protection around their mind, body, and souls from the enemy. Oh Lord, Father, I bind every attack of the enemy against the minds and souls of your children, and I unleash Your wrath toward anything or anybody that exalts itself against You and The Kingdom of God. Father, I declare healing, restoration, positioning, prosperity, and Your purpose be done in the lives of Your children. In Jesus Name, I pray...Amen.

Blocked Broken Blessed

SHAWNA D. BRACKENS

"Now faith is the substance of things hoped for, the evidence of things not seen."

—Hebrews 11:1 KJV

"Whatever the mind can conceive and believe, it can achieve."

—Napoleon Hill

Let it be, let it be, let it be, let it be. There will be an answer, let it be.

As The Beatles album played, children sang along at the top of their lungs. I was teaching in Korea at the time and the English festival was one day away. The dress rehearsal meant no one was leaving until every presentation was perfect. As they continued repeating the chorus of this song, I found myself singing along.

There will be an answer, let it be. Yes, there will be an answer let it be.

I walked home from work that evening feeling like heaven had come down and ministered to me through this song. It was a confirmation for the question I had posed to

God earlier in the week. And for further validation, I received a large goodie box from my sister in Florida, full of motivational posters, candy, stickers, workbooks, and supplies for my students.

It is important to look for answers to problems in unusual places. Be open to receive a response to your prayer, however it shows up.

It was settled. I was going to begin my weight release journey with the expectation that I would achieve success. I'd begin by replacing negative thoughts with positive ones, and I would read as much as I could about weight reduction, body types, and meal selections in order to succeed. And of course, I would petition God to guide me as I trusted in Him:

> *Lord, is it possible for me to lose weight? Even though I have a few health challenges that medical journals say should be prevent me from doing so? Lord, You are the Great Physician. And because I am fearfully and wonderfully made, I accept whatever is meant to be for my life. You are the Source of total supply of healing, help, and hope. Guide me, O Great Jehovah. Make straight the path for my feet. Forgive me for any and all harm that I have brought on myself by making unhealthy eating choices. Reveal to me any hidden blocks, unguarded thoughts, traumatic events, or words that have been spoken over me or to me that I have unconsciously tucked away. Allow me to progress in this new weight release journey. I surrender to You. In Jesus' Name, Amen.*

It is so important to consult the Lord regarding any major life changes. It's also equally important to ask for forgiveness and mercy to correct any misguided thoughts or actions that hinder personal growth.

Just as I was preparing to begin my weight loss journey in 1997, my plans came to a screeching halt. I had visited the doctor for what I thought was a bad sore throat. The physician felt my neck and said, "This is more than a sore throat. Go immediately to the hospital for tests and x-rays. I highly suspect this hard knot is cancer. It's not moving."

"What?" I exclaimed. "You're wrong. Can I just have antibiotics to kill the bacteria?"

He ignored my pleas, and the tests confirmed his prognosis. I was diagnosed with invasive cancer of the thyroid. I had a portion of my thyroid removed, along with a malignant tumor the size of a small tangerine. This shocked my internal system in such a way that I gained thirty pounds in a short period of time. Not only was my hormonal balance out of whack, my metabolism became sluggish and my remaining thyroid function was low to none. I was initially put on medicine and told I would have to take it for the rest of my life to balance things out. I quit it after about six months. I couldn't seem the get the dosage right, and the side effects of mood swings, swelling, night sweats, heart palpitations, weeping, and restlessness were outweighing the perceived benefits. I wanted to lose weight but my body needed healing first.

Both my surgeon and my family doctor told me I would gain weight and it would be nearly impossible to get it off. I believed them. It never dawned upon me to question them. Since that time, I have learned the importance of conducting personal research regarding any medical conditions, diagnosis, treatments, etc. Have you ever received a diagnosis of any sort? Please do your own adequate research and get a second opinion. It helps to be in the know when facing major or minor medical decisions.

The second medical scare to exacerbate my weight gain happened in 1999. That's the year I had to have an emergency radical surgery to induce menopause in order to save my life. Prior to the surgery, I experienced massive blood loss daily. Some mornings, I could actually scoop up piles of congealed blood from my bed with my hands. By the time I got to the hospital that hot summer day, I knew something was seriously wrong. It was a blistering 99 degrees but I was freezing cold, shivering as it if were a cold winter day. I covered myself with a warm blanket to stop the shivering, but it didn't work.

It turned out that my blood count was dangerously low, and the doctor said I needed emergency surgery. I was given three units of blood before the surgery could even begin. They asked me if I had blacked out or had any fainting spells in the weeks leading up to surgery, which I hadn't, and they seemed surprised. During the surgery, I required two more pints of blood and one more afterwards. Afterwards, my surgeon told me he was 99% sure I had cancer again since there were numerous suspicious masses in various areas of my body, but we would have to wait until the test results came back to be sure. The reports came back all negative. No evidence of the disease. Thanks be unto God for this victory.

I spent the next twelve days in the hospital. The first four days, I was heavily sedated, drifting in and out of consciousness, and on the morphine pump. On day five, I remember waking up and feeling like an eighteen-wheeler had run over my guts, backed up, and parked. The pain was excruciating. On the day I was released, I couldn't go to my house. I needed more time to recuperate. So, my parents took me to their home and helped me get well for another four weeks. About two months later, I felt a lot better. But I had gained another twenty pounds.

During my post-op follow-up, my surgeon seemed surprised and happy that none of the masses that he'd found and removed from my body were malignant. He also indicated that, because of my excess "visceral situation," his cuts had to be deeper and the healing would take longer. He also had to use extra surgical staples to hold my abdomen together, and some would need to stay in longer. I think regular people who have similar surgeries usually require 24 to 26. Me? I had 54 surgical clamps holding me together. Yep! My stomach was huge.

Despite the fact that I was heavier than a sumo wrestler and weighed more than a baby elephant does at birth, no one ever teased me about being fat. The only thing I remember is one of my brothers saying that, if I ever won the lottery, they'd probably find me in alley overdosed on food! Now, that was really funny. He was a comedian, and I did love to eat. I was just happy to be alive and my size was the last thing on my mind.

Fast forward to 2008. I was ready to live my dream of being an international educator in Asia. God was bringing into fruition a dream I'd had since the age of tender age of three-years-old. I had accepted a position to work as an educator in Korea. My online research had indicated to me that Koreans don't like fat people. In fact, in Korea, fat people are considered, lazy, irresponsible, uneducated, and unattractive. I'd even read that a few instructors had been left at the airport by the employer, after they'd seen their shape, size, or color. Wow!

There was no way I was going to change colors, lose half of my weight, or make my shape transform into some visually pleasing image overnight. So, once again, I found myself at the foot of the cross, seeking out my Soul Source.

Dear God,
Thank You for being the Source of my total supply. Thank You in advance for allowing me to walk in peace, victory, and unusual favor upon my arrival to Korea. Once again, I ask You to make straight the path for my feet. O Lord, I am grateful to be fearfully and wonderfully made. In Jesus' Name, Amen.

My worries melted into joy and relief upon arriving at the international airport in Korea. As soon as my boss saw me, the first words out of his mouth were, "I like you already!" All 330 pounds had been favored. Nobody could have done that but God. Please recognize that, when the hand of the Lord is upon your life and He is truly ordering your steps, all people, places, and things will have to line up with His plan and purpose.

So what happened next? One Sunday, I happened upon a wonderful little church in Seoul. The pastors were kind prayer warriors, who prayed several hours a day. One of them, Pastor Jang, looked at me and said, "This sickness is not unto death. God is going to remove the blocks." At that point, I was totally happy, well, and getting along just fine. The "sickness" she was referencing was my fat body. She said that there was no way I could be this fat and not be sick, and that God was going to remove the "blocks." How could this lady tell me I was fat and sick? Didn't she know I had a slow metabolism, a sluggish thyroid, was postmenopausal, and a cancer survivor? Who says that? Apparently someone who is led by the Spirit to help you get to the root of a problem. I told her that I was healthy, happy, and holding onto my fat for dear life.

"Skinny people die faster in a famine," I said and walked out the door. Of course, I returned, just not that day. Thank God for mercy. When God sends you a seasoned word from someone you know is a true prayer warrior, receive it. Don't reject it because it stings. He speaks in mysterious ways. He can use anybody and anything to get your attention.

I went home and stretched out on the floor. In the old days, we called it lying prostrate before the Lord. I surrendered my list of excuses and asked God to show me what was blocking me from losing weight and to take away any false assumptions. He took me to that place. He brought up painful memories. This is my first time sharing them.

For years, I had blamed my weight gain on a slow metabolism, hereditary fat genes, low functioning thyroid, cancer, menopause, and surgery. In actuality, those things had little or nothing to with it. I am sure of this now. Regardless of what you've been told, always thought, or imagined about the why behind your "extra fluff," when the uncomfortable truth comes up, own it. Otherwise, you'll always live in a comfortable lie.

What was the real root of my being so comfortable using morbid obesity like a security blanket? Everyone has a reason. Find the "blocks" and your breakthrough will follow. Two submerged memories were uncovered for me. One block occurred when I was in the first grade. The other happened in senior high school.

Tuesday, January 1, 1975: It was in the middle of the night. I heard a commotion and jumped up to see what was happening. I was five and curious. I could see everyone clearly but no one saw me. And then it happened. While my father went outside to warm up the station wagon and my mother went to the closet to get a coat. I heard my sister let out a deep sigh and fall dead on the floor. When my dad returned, he scooped her up from the yellow linoleum floor, wrapped her in a blanket, and carried her out the back door. And I never saw her again.

Earlier, I had heard my older brother say, "Momma, come quick. Something is wrong with Marilyn. She's breathing funny." Momma helped Marilyn to the kitchen by the door.

She said, "Marilyn, hold on a second. Let me get your coat. It's freezing outside."

Marilyn looked at mom and said, "Okay." I heard Marilyn speak.

Meanwhile my father had rushed outside to get the old station wagon cranked up. In the blink of an eye, Marilyn let out one final gasp and dropped. My parents returned to the kitchen at the same time to see their precious young fourteen-year-old daughter lying on the kitchen floor, limp and lifeless, her eyes rolled back in her head.

"Marilyn Ann, Marilyn Ann," I heard my father say. "Oh, Marilyn Ann is gone." As they took her out, I heard them say, "She was just too skinny. She was just too skinny."

I could see tears falling down my mother's cheeks, but she was careful not to make a sound. She didn't want to wake the rest of the children. After that, I tiptoed back to my bed and had a nightmare. I never told anyone what I saw that night.

The next day, we didn't go to school. I asked where Marilyn was and when she was coming back. Our parents gathered the family together in the living room and told us what had happened. Marilyn had suffered a fatal sickle cell crisis in the middle of the night and she didn't make it through. I wanted to yell out, "She died because she was too skinny!" But I didn't. The day after Marilyn died, we started eating a lot more food at each meal. Momma said she wanted everyone to have some meat on their bones. She started cooking double and we started eating double. Double everything.

From the very moment Marilyn died, the one comment that attached itself to my psyche, lodged itself into my subconscious, and created a false narrative was this: "She was just too skinny." As I grew older, I would see skinny people and think, "They're going to drop dead." A plump person, on the other hand, was going to live because they were strong and healthy.

The second "block" happened my senior year in high school. I arrived home to a message that one of the ministers at the church wanted to meet with me at his home. It was urgent. He felt "led" to have a talk with me. I was surprised since he seldom even talked to me at church. When I arrived, a guest evangelist was also there. Our church was in the midst of a revival. The evangelist said he was concerned that I might end up "missing out" on Heaven. I sat there in shock, wondering where all of this coming from.

In summary, he said that my body was a source of temptation to many men. He said my chest area was big and my hips were shapely and I had a small waist. And this combination would cause me to "miss heaven," if I succumbed to the desires of the new converts that I was bringing to church each day. As silly as this all sounds now, at the time, I was terrified. He proceeded to tell me that, while I was busy saving others, I would become a castaway if I didn't do something about my body. The local minister agreed with his assessment. They volunteered to pray with me. I thanked them, received their prayers, and returned home to get ready for church. For the record, I never succumbed to any temptations of new converts I was bringing to church, because there weren't any "converts." When guys used to invite me out, I'd reply, "Sure! Only if I get to pick the place." And then I'd bring them to church instead of going on a real date.

That same day, I started dressing like an old lady and eating as much food as I could to gain weight (and I did), so my shape would disappear and I wouldn't "miss heaven." Within six months, I gained about sixty pounds. Later, I learned that the evangelist was the one with issues and had been spilling his seed across the country. Isn't this what psychologists call "projecting?"

Stand firm in your holy conviction. Don't be bullied by a spiritual leader or someone who is supposedly looking out for your soul. Use discernment and common sense when dealing with someone who claims to speak for God.

That day in 2009, when Pastor Jang called me out and prayed that the blocks would be moved, was one of the best days of my life. I found the "blocks" and asked God to remove them from me. I wanted a lifestyle change that reflected self-care for my temple, so I began to lose weight effectively and consistently. My breakthrough came when I accepted the uncomfortable truth in place of a comfortable lie.

Today, I am healed, healthy, and whole. The blocks have been broken by the power of prayer, and I have successfully released and kept off about 130 pounds for more than four years. I see my waist coming back. And the journey continues.

May this story help you find answers in difficult places. God can only heal what you're willing to reveal. Be open to hear His voice in any way He chooses to speak. Whether it's a song, a quote, a prayer, or a prophetic voice, or even a story in this book, listen and respond accordingly. You are not alone in your struggle. Somebody, somewhere has experienced the same pain and come out victoriously. Instead of spending time thinking about why you can't, use that same mental energy to think of as many ways that you can. Recognize and eliminate fear. Gather tips, tools, and techniques to assist you on your journey.

Make today a day of prayer to break the "block" and be willing to do whatever is necessary to move forward, even if it's uncomfortable and painful. Trust the process of life. Not everything in and of itself is going to be good, but it's working for your good. Someone needs to hear your story. Tell it as a victor not as a victim. Get a spiritual foundation so that you can build your faith on a solid Soul Source.

At the end of the day, life doesn't happen to you, you happen to it.

"God grant me the serenity to accept the things I cannot change. Courage to change the things I can. And wisdom to know the difference."

— Prayer of St. Francis of Assisi

Seed of My Father

TANEISHA MITCHELL

"And I will restore to you the years that the locust have eaten, the cankerworm and the caterpillar, and the palmerworm, my great army which I sent among you."

—Joel 2:25

"There is not greater agony than bearing an untold story inside of you."

—Maya Angelou

Like most people, I wondered why my life had to be so hard at times. Why me? But then again, why not me? I had always been kind, compassionate, and loving, and, at the same time, a no-nonsense type of person. You had to be, especially growing up in the streets of West Philadelphia. I've had to fist fight from the first grade to the initial years of college, so I'm used to a good fight. Even once I moved away, when I came home to visit Philadelphia, there was a fight bound to be lurking around the corner, waiting for my arrival.

I was in the first grade when I got in my first fight. A boy in my class decided he was going to pull one of my ponytails so hard that I thought my neck would pop off! He must have lost his mind. My reaction was not to cry like most girls would do at age six. Nope, he didn't know who he was messing with—I hauled off and punched him right in his face as hard as I could. He fell out of the chair, his face turned red as a beet, and he started crying. The whole room went silent in shock.

I stood over top of him proudly, almost daring him to get up. Our teacher pulled me out of the way and scolded me for hitting him so hard. She cuddled him like he was a baby. I tried to explain to her that he started it but she didn't want to hear it. I thought to myself, "I bet he will never pull another girl's hair again." But I was also embarrassed and hurt that the teacher scolded me in front of everyone. I wanted to cry but I knew not to show any hurt or tears in front of others. My uncles taught me better.

My two uncles were only four and six years older than me, and they taught me a lot of lessons early in life during their bullying sessions. One rule I learned quickly was to never let them see me cry. If a tear welled in my eyes, it would bring about long, mimicking rants. They would put their faces close enough that I could feel their hot breath and spit splatter on my face as they screamed crying sounds as loud as they could: "Whaa whaa whaa, listen to the baby! Whaa whaa whaa, come change the baby's diaper!"

If I didn't suck the tears up and wipe my face right away, they would yell and stomp their feet like command sergeants and demand that I stop crying right now, and most importantly, to stop acting like a damn girl! I began to believe that crying was bad and that there was definitely something wrong with "acting" like a girl or showing any signs of vulnerability.

They continued their mission to break me out of acting like a girl by making me fight. They would make me fight any little boy younger than them or who was too small for them to fight. If I refused to fight or didn't win the fight convincingly, they would put their funky, dirty feet in my face or my mouth while I slept, which, by the way, gave me a foot phobia for over twenty years. If it wasn't a foot in my mouth, it was hot sauce on my lips. When I would wake with lips burning, they would offer me some water but it would be scolding hot.

To toughen up my fists or make my knuckles bigger, they forced me to play the card game "Knucks." All I remember is them hitting my knuckles as hard as they could with a deck of cards over and over again, and I wasn't supposed to cry. My knuckles would turn bright red and swell. I had to keep all these sessions secret so they wouldn't get in trouble and torture me more. I decided at a very young age that it was necessary to keep secrets, not show emotions, and be tough like a boy in order to survive. The little boy in my first grade class didn't know who he had hit.

After being humiliated by the teacher, I asked if I could go to the bathroom. When she gave me permission, instead of going to the bathroom, I ran out the side door of the school. I scaled the school's side windows and climbed over the fence so I could run home across the street and tell my mom what happen. My grandmother was shocked to see me home so early. I told her what happened but she didn't seem to care much about the scuffle. She was more concerned that I left school property during school hours. She called my mother, and when my she came home early, I told her what had happened and got the response I was looking for.

She said, "That is what the hell he deserved and I'll bet he thinks twice before he pulls someone else's hair." She went on to say, "And if someone puts their hands on you again, you better hit them back twice as much and twice as hard. You better always protect yourself. If I hear you let someone do something to you and you didn't fight back, I'm going to beat your butt myself, so you better take your chances with them." She had no idea her two youngest brothers were torturing and bullying me almost daily. She walked me back across the street to school and wished any adult would tell her that I was wrong for defending myself.

My early childhood experiences literally shaped me into a woman who was afraid (more like terrified) to embrace vulnerability or femininity. I thought being perceived as tough was far better than being perceived as weak. Don't get me wrong: I had no issues with looking like a beautiful woman. On the outside, I always kept my hair done and my appointment was set for once a week. I always wore the sharpest clothes and stayed on a diet to fit in those sharp clothes. I used the strength that bullying ignited in me to walk with confidence and not be intimidated by anyone. I asked the questions that others were afraid to ask and never worried about whether others liked me or not. Being bullied taught me to be self-sufficient and, more importantly, made me despise any type of bullying done to others. I found myself in fights or arguments that had nothing to do with me, because I innately found it necessary to bring bullies to justice and stand up for someone who otherwise couldn't. I had no tolerance for any picking on or abuse.

As I got older, girlfriends knew just who to call if there was ever any drama. They would call after a physical altercation with a boyfriend, and I would stop whatever I was doing and go to wherever my friend was and ask her boyfriend to give me just one minute so I could show him a thing or two. I started to wonder to myself if all men beat on their women in some form or fashion; it seemed to be happening everywhere I turned. I found myself telling my girlfriends exactly where to hit a man to bring him to his knees, and it wasn't the private area—it was his Adams apple. Hit a man across the Adams apple and he will stop breathing for a minute or two.

I would give them all relationship advice that I never took for myself. I explained what they should and should not tolerate and how to protect their hearts from the unfaithful ways of men. One of my go-to advice for when boyfriends cheated was to be just as unfaithful to them in return, because then, it wouldn't hurt as bad when you found out about their wrong doings. All this advice came from a bitter, broken place in my heart, not a love space at all. My friends told me all the time that I thought and acted like men did, and it didn't bother me that they felt that way. I just figured it was because I grew up as the only girl amongst six group home boys. As a result of my upbringing, I never needed a man like my girlfriends did, though I was always in some sort of relationship.

Somewhere along the way, I became everyone's illegitimate counselor and protector as if I were actually qualified to do so. I spent all this energy on everyone else's problems while, on the inside, I was just as lost and broken as they were. I was fighting demons and abuse too; I was just a better actress than they were, with different coping skills. Nobody provided me counseling or protected me—I had to rely on my strength. Only later did I realize that my strength was just for survival; it was merely superficial. It had to be: I didn't know God personally at the time and I didn't depend on Him the way I should have or could have. I was arrogant enough to think I had all these things under control. I couldn't have been more wrong.

Are you trying to play the role of God in other people's lives? Are you trying to be the fixer of all things? Are you trying to be the protector or the counselor for any and everyone in your circle who rings your phone? If you honestly evaluate your role in relationships and can answer yes to any one of these questions, do yourself a favor and free yourself—it is not your assignment. Of course, it is perfectly fine to help people, and to be kind and supportive, but it's not okay to become the God in their lives. You can't fix them or their problems.

Give these assignments you have placed on yourself to God before He shows you that only He is God and in full control of all things. Only He is the alpha and the omega, the beginning and the end, the healer and the redeemer. I got to see who God was firsthand in one of the most terrifying nights of my life. My days of acting like a man, acting like a counselor, and acting like a protector came to a halt right after a close friend of mine decided to tell my husband I was having an affair. I had justified my affair with excuses—"What's good for the goose is good for the gander," "I have forgiven him but I will never forget what he has done," and "He doesn't love me anymore anyway." I reminded myself often of my vow to never be the type of woman who would love a man so much that it would break me down, almost to the point of wanting to commit suicide. I would never allow my daughter to fall to her knees with tears running down her face, wrapping her arms around my waist and begging me not to pull the trigger of a loaded gun, all over an affair that breaks my heart.

I made all the excuses in the world that I could possibly think of in order to keep my heart shielded and not commit to giving anyone my full heart. Are you making excuses for yourself to not give 100% of your heart to anyone the way God intended for us to love? When our hearts are shielded, love can't get in or out.

For over twenty-five years, my brokenness was masked under false strength. After witnessing the strongest woman in the world to me become broken and contemplate suicide over an affair, I was unwilling to accept vulnerability or release my shielded heart. This theory led to being in multiple failed relationships and ultimately a marriage in which I never fully knew how to commit without fear. I was afraid of being vulnerable, terrified to even say the word. I had to protect my heart. When I watched my mother lose all emotional control after my father's affair, I vowed to never give any man my whole heart. If the greatest man in the world couldn't be trusted, how could any other man? Even when God sent me the man I was praying for, my husband, I didn't recognize his love as true and, when I started to see it as pure love, it wasn't normal for me. I decided to sabotage it with my own affair to get back to my dysfunctional normal. Could you be living in a dysfunctional normal?

My affair did not make my husband contemplate suicide at all. It caused him to contemplate murder. In a dark voice, one that I could barely recognize, my husband confronted me about the suspected affair. It was close to two in the morning and we were home alone with no one there to witness what might have been the end of my life. Before he reached behind his back, before I ever saw the gun, I could sense danger in the room. I had a feeling like a scared gazelle has before the lion attacks. I wanted to run away but his broad body was blocking the door. I wanted to scream but no one would have heard me any way. He grabbed me and put the silver gun to my head. I was in total shock. I felt my body tremble and I struggled to breathe. The affair was already over so how could he have found out?

I was frozen; no words were coming out of my mouth. If I could speak, my answer would have been "No" but he wouldn't have believed me anyway. All I could do was cry out and beg God to please help me. I didn't want my life to end this way. In that moment, He spoke, "You are not being the daughter I created you to be. You cannot run from love. Stop it." All I could mutter with the lump in my throat was, "I am Sorry. Please forgive me." I don't know if I was speaking to God, my husband, or myself in that moment but all three of us deserved an apology.

My prayers were answered when my husband put the gun down as tears welled in his eyes. I knew that I had finally broken the wrong man's heart. I felt like the lowest human being on earth as he reminded me that the only thing he asked me to do was to never hurt him. He said, "From the day I fell in love with you, I said, whatever you do, just don't hurt me, and you promised you would never hurt me." I had broken the ultimate promise to him and now I wanted to be forgiven—something I have never sought before.

God had ended the affair I was in just as fast as it started. But it lingered in the air long enough for my friend to tell my husband all the makings of what I shared with her. She wanted my husband for herself and figured that being the messenger of these indiscretions would surely place my husband in her arms instead of mine. She convinced herself that I didn't deserve a man like my husband and she would know exactly how to treat him. But what she didn't know or realize was that I am highly favored and no weapon formed against me shall prosper. She didn't realize that no man can come between who God has brought together as husband and wife. She did not know or realize that I was a blessed seed of my Father—but it wasn't her fault. How could she know any of these things when I didn't know these things to be true for myself?

God was not going to allow my life to end over an affair caused by brokenness and confusion. He wanted to show me that I wasted so many years of my life running from my true self and running from the love that He placed in my heart for myself and others. By not embracing who He created me to be, I went head first towards falsehood and destruction.

I know this because, as my husband held the gun to my head, I had an out-of-body experience. I was there but I wasn't there. I could see my mother, twenty years ago, holding the gun to her own head. We were both in the same place. In that moment, I cried out to God to help me and I understood the lesson. I would never fail love again. The generational curse of affairs and a fear of loving with a full heart stops with me. My daughter will not face that enemy.

Today, I am more than excited to know there is a restoration occurring in my life. I no longer suppress the loving, faithful, and vulnerable woman who God created me to be, and neither should you. I have learned to embrace my femininity and vulnerability. In my most vulnerable moments, I actually show my true strength and courage by letting them come through. My vulnerability is like a breath of fresh air and a freedom that I can now feel running through my veins. I no longer keep my heart shielded or stay in protection mode. I give it to God first.

I no longer try to be the second man in my marriage. I have submitted my life to my husband, and I am no longer his bully, I am only his complement. I understand that God used my husband and my friend to save my life. My afflictions were good for me and necessary to grow into the woman God created me to be. My husband was the only man who could show me what unconditional love truly looks like. It is so easy to say, "I forgive but I won't forget" until you are the one seeking forgiveness for yourself and from someone you love. To truly forgive in a Christ-like manner is to forgive as if the act never occurred.

We have to learn to be merciful to others and not only accept God's Grace, but we also have to learn to give grace away to others whenever and wherever it is required. Why not start with the ones you love and let them see the seed of our father God in you? When I look back on my relationship with my husband now, I don't have to wonder how we made it through the darkest places of our lives; I know it was only because of God's love and covenant over our union that we continue to celebrate years in a loving marriage. There is one scripture that comes to my mind repeatedly when I think of God's love for us, First Corinthians 13:4:

> *"Love is patient and kind; love does not envy or boast; it is not arrogant or rude. It does not insist on its own way it is not irritable or resentful, it does not rejoice at wrongdoing but rejoices with the truth. Love bears all things, believes all things, hopes all things, and endures all things. Love never fails."*

Thank you, Dear Lord, for my restoration—my later days will be my brighter days. My prayer for others is that my journey will somehow help you find a way to embrace the very thing you are running from. It very well may be the thing that is meant to save your life.

Facing Grief with God's Grace

KIM FRANCIS

"Blessed are those who mourn, for they shall be comforted."
—Matthew 5:4

"He is committed to making even the worst moments in your life result in good."
—Romans 8:28

Everyone at some point in their lives will experience tremendous and profound loss. It is inescapable, and yet, nothing really truly prepares you for it until the day it arrives. I found there are many definitions of grief but the one I most relate to is "a multifaceted response to loss, particularly to the loss of someone or something that has died, to which a bond or affection was formed. Although conventionally focused on the emotional response to loss, it also has physical, cognitive, behavioral, social, and philosophical dimensions."

My profound loss occurred on March 29, 2015, the day my beautiful mom passed away from her year-long battle with esophageal cancer and the day a new companion named grief entered by life. Since that day, I have broken my life into two acronyms, BMPA (Before Mom Passed Away) and AMPA (After Mom Passed Away).

I always felt that I was prepared for anything life threw at me because my beautiful, resilient, and vibrant mom was by my side and would be there to love, encourage, and push me through as she had so many times before. Yet nothing ever prepared me for life without her. What I can say for sure is that I will continue to experience and learn many lessons from my grief companion until the day my time on earth is through and I'm reunited with her in heaven. I find peace often when reading 2 Peter 1:3: "And he will give you everything you need to face whatever you encounter in this fallen world, even death."

To know my mom was to love her, and she was loved by so many people. I know from experience and from those of others that she could be very intimidating at times because she never held anything back about how she felt. You always knew where you stood with her and I always admired her for that characteristic. If you remember Stockard Channing's role as Betty Rizzo in the movie *Grease*, then you can get a better sense of who my Mom was as a person. She was stunning and turned heads with her big brown eyes and dark brownish-black hair which, depending on the day or month, may have been streaked with pink or purple, or better yet, she might have completely transformed herself into a platinum blonde or a ruby redhead. She always said that that was the beautician inside of her. We used to laugh often about how her need to change hairstyles flowed into her changing the colors of the walls and decorative themes in our house. We never knew what to expect when we entered her home or saw her next: Her home was always a work of art and she looked like a million bucks.

Sue Ann Giles (Rohrbough) was born on May 7, 1951 and, like Rizzo, she smoked, cussed, enjoyed sarcasm and a good laugh, and was tough as nails. She used to say she was street smart compared to my being book smart. She had me when she was sixteen so, in a sense, we grew up together. There is a fifteen-year difference between my youngest brother, Garrett, and I, so as I grew older, I admired her even more when I thought about the challenges, courage, and strength it must have taken to be a teenager herself raising a daughter. She was an excellent mother who had fierce loyalty to her children. She was the first to admit when she made mistakes but we always knew she loved us and could make us laugh (after she roared, of course).

Mom loved exploring flea markets and thrift stores. She couldn't wait to call or show me the bargains she found at Goodwill, the Resale Barn, or The Crowded Closet, where she worked and volunteered designing their windows into themes from the donations. She had such a true gift for designing and decorating. Many of her friends would hire her to come redo their homes and she loved shopping for each project, looking for just the right colors or pieces she created on her mental canvas. She always knew exactly what she needed or wanted to make it perfect.

Mom was diagnosed with stage-four esophageal cancer in March 2014. I silently screamed inside when we received the news, and yet, truly believed she was going to beat it because Mom was a warrior. She was already a two-time cancer survivor and I knew: If anyone could kick cancer's rear end, it was her. Knowing the intensity of the treatment plan and the battle she faced, my brother and his wife had "Team Sue" bracelets made for everyone with the Bible verse Deuteronomy 31:6: "Be strong and courageous. Do not be afraid or terrified because of them, for the Lord your God goes with you; he will never leave you or forsake you."

Watching her fight this vile disease and seeing the impact the chemotherapy and radiation had on her body was more than I could bear, yet I never wanted her to know how much emotional pain I was in as I watched her endure all of the side effects. I was determined to never let her see me cry but I spent many nights after she went to bed, crying, praying, and pleading with God to please heal her. I will forever be in awe and admiration of her courage and the warrior strength she displayed despite the tremendous amount of pain and discomfort she was in. She got up every single day and was a shining example of grace and class through every step. In fact, when people saw her out in the community, they would comment on how beautiful she looked and, if they didn't know about her cancer, they would have never known she was sick.

Sadly, after a year into the valiant and courageous battle, Mom went to be with the Lord as the song "The Old Rugged Cross" played and I stood at her bedside, holding her hand. I kept telling her over and over how proud I was of her, that I would be sure to take care of my brother Joey, and how exciting it would be to have Grandma and the angels meet her at the gates of heaven to see our Lord Jesus Christ and welcome her home. Up until the moment she passed, I had prayed and believed she would be healed. I wouldn't let myself think otherwise. And then, my beautiful mom, best friend, and rock was gone. Grief immediately consumed me. I will never forget the deep heart-wrenching sorrow and the indescribable pain of losing her. That day has forever changed me. It also changed the way I view life, things, people, family, and friends. An important lesson I learned was that none of us are guaranteed tomorrow so we should live in the present and tell others how we much we appreciate and love them.

Regardless of how unexpected or predictable, death shakes us to the core. The pain is inescapable, leaving us with feelings of absolute emptiness and pure devastation. Yet Jesus promised in Matthew 5:4, "Blessed are those who mourn, for they shall be comforted." God beckons us into His loving arms so He can heal our wounded hearts.

My heart struggled to make sense of the loss. I went into emotional shock as anxiety, fear, and fatigue took their toll on me. Grief became a weight. Grief became pain. Grief became physical. My mind and body fell apart. At times, the sheer act of breathing in and out felt like I was climbing a mountain. During the first few months, I prayed multiple times a day, asking God to give me the strength to just put one foot in front of the other. It was several months until I felt like I could breathe fully without restrictions.

Coping with the loss of someone we love is one of life's biggest challenges. The pain feels so overwhelming and causes such deep and profound sadness that it can disrupt our physical health, making it difficult to sleep, eat, or even think straight. These are all normal reactions to significant loss. The mourning process is not just for the loss of the person we loved but it's also for the loss of ourselves. Who we were before their passing will never return because life without them is forever different. Yet, we must experience the pain of loss: We can't avoid it, go around it, over it, or under it, as much as we would like to. The only way out is through. I remember repeating Philippians 4:13 over and over again, and I still do many times a week: "I can do all things through Christ who gives me strength.".

At times, I felt so lost, like I wasn't making any progress at all. I knew I was at a crossroads in life, but I often found myself asking what I wanted to do with the rest of my life. Picking up the pieces hasn't been easy but God has never left me and continues to provide the resources I need to move ahead and find the key to life and living again without Mom. Proverbs 3: 5-6 reminds me to "Trust in the LORD with all your heart and lean not on your own understanding but in all your ways submit to him and he will make your paths straight."

I have learned to never allow myself to get stuck in the danger of despair. I was for a long time and realized that it wasn't what Mom would have wanted for me. How could I truly celebrate and honor her if I remained stuck in the trap of grief? The loss was defining my life instead of *me* defining my life.

As we face the death of our loved ones, it is so important to remember you are not alone. Jesus endured death for us so that, even in the face of death ourselves, we would be able to live with hope, strength, and courage. Good things can happen, even in the darkest moments of life, so we can't let grief rob us of living. As hard as it is, we must choose to live and experience the grace that Jesus died to give us.

I will share from my experience that, if there is ever a time you need to set realistic expectations for yourself, it is during the most intense time of your grieving. Throw away the timelines: It truly is one day at a time. Don't let anyone try to squeeze you into their expectations of what grief should be or how you should feel. Express yourself in a way that is right for you, and be patient with yourself. Be patient with those who don't understand, which may include your own family. Your grief is your own and no one else can tell you when it's time to "move on" or "get over it." Honor yourself and your feelings. Feel through those moments of overwhelming sadness or when the tears will not stop falling. Keep reminding yourself that it is normal to feel this way—*you are normal* and it will be okay. Let yourself feel without embarrassment or judgment. It's okay to be angry, to yell at the heavens, to cry, or not to cry. It's also okay to laugh, to find moments of joy, and to let go when you're ready.

God doesn't want us to hide our emotions or wear a happy face, pretending we are alright if we aren't. He wants us to go to Him with complete honesty, as he states in the Psalms. He knows us completely and loves us unconditionally. 1 Peter 5:7 says "Cast all your anxieties on him because he cares for you." I have seen in my moments of complete darkness, little lights of God's grace and love shine through. Search for the light. Pay attention to the little things God is doing: "For we walk by faith, not by sight" (2 Corinthians 5:7). Many times since Mom's passing, I felt God saying to me, "Rest in Me. You have journeyed up a steep and rugged path. The way ahead is shrouded with uncertainty. Don't look behind you or ahead of you. Stay focused on Me in the here and now. Trust Me that I will equip you with the tools you need for your journey ahead. Remember I am with you, watching over you wherever you go"

Like I said before, there is no timetable for grief. We can't schedule how long it's going to take to get "through it." In fact, I believe we will *never* get "through it." I will always be a bereaved person. Mom will never be "here" again in this life, and the finality of that statement still causes me to tear up. I will always be "in the process," but I am learning to embrace it, work through it, and allow myself to heal the hurt, so that I can keep moving on with my life in full light and recognition of what's happened and watch God change my life as a result.

I've always heard from books and in conversation that the first year of grieving is the hardest. I know for myself that navigating through the first birthdays and holidays without Mom were excruciatingly painful and I spent many months in a blur of shock and disbelief that she was really gone. The assumption for some I have talked to is that time passed should make the days and years ahead easier. For me, it's coming up on two years since Mom went to heaven and I still have many hard days. And yet, I work to adjust my focus on her being with me always instead of my living without her. I am choosing now to see the beauty surrounding me each day and smiling more often as I think of her and what I would say if she was here. At times, I still talk to her in the car or while I am walking as if she was on the phone or sitting with me as we did for so many years.

When my Grandma died, I gave Mom a framed poem, "Do Not Stand At My Grave and Weep" by Mary Elizabeth Fry. Little did I know then how important this poem would be to me when I lost Mom, and I often share it with others who experience loss in their lives:

> Do not stand at my grave and weep
> I am not there. I do not sleep.
> I am a thousand winds that blow.
> I am the diamond glints on snow.
> I am the sun on ripened grain.
> I am the gentle autumn rain.
> When you awaken in the morning's hush
> I am the swift uplifting rush
> Of quiet birds in circled flight.
> I am the soft stars that shine at night.
> Do not stand at my grave and cry;
> I am not there. I did not die.

There is no love as pure, unconditional, and strong as a mother's love. There is a void inside of me that will always be present, and those feelings will never go away. However, I am learning to live with them and smile again. Those who know me well would say I have made significant progress over the last twenty-four months, despite many of the other unspoken crosses of pain and rejection I have carried. In the midst of my pain, I have learned to laugh again. I have learned to accept joy. I am continuously learning how to navigate through this world as a motherless daughter. I fall at times, but I always get up. I make a choice to rise because I am my mother's daughter and a child of God, and giving up is not an option. I can hear Mom's voice saying to me during the difficult days, "Rise up, Kimberly. You can do this."

Her life brings me so much joy. As I climb out of the pit of grief, I realize how very blessed and grateful I am to have had sixty-three years with her, because I know there are many girls and women in this world who never knew their Mom or lost them way too soon. I cherish the laughter, the fun memories, the lessons, the tears, the trips, the last months holding her hand or rubbing her back and talking about her life, her childhood, her greatest accomplishments, her regrets—there are just so many moments which can never be taken away from me. I focus on that every day and burst with pride inside because I'm her daughter, guided and influenced by her to be the woman I am today.

For the rest of my life, I will celebrate her through my life. I'm her legacy and there is peace knowing a part of her will always be inside of me. At times, I feel her spirit cheering me on. I catch myself saying something and laughing because it's exactly what she would have said. I visit a thrift store and pick something up, knowing she would have loved it too. Many of her friends tell me, "You sound just like your mother" or "Your expressions and or laughter remind me so much of your mom." And I smile because I feel her in those moments. I am determined now more than ever to carry on her legacy of service to others.

This journey with grief is far from over, but I am here to tell you that we can make it. We find strength in the weakness, joy in the pain, laughter in tears. Yes, we will see the world through a different set of eyes after the loss but we will make it with God's grace. I trust God to bring me out on the other side, stronger with a deeper and abiding faith. Never give up on the love and bond you shared with your loved one. It surrounds us every day and lives on forever. I know the love Mom and I have is eternal and will never die. And I know, one day, I will be more than just okay: "Those who sow with tears will reap with songs of joy" (Psalm 126:5).

Forgiveness Gave Me the Power to Live and Love Completely

DENISE POLOTE-KELLY

And when you stand praying, if you hold anything against anyone, forgive him, so that your Father in heaven may forgive you your sins.

—Mark 11:25

When I think back and detail the order of my life, I now see that, for me to live and love completely and to forgive others, I had to truly forgive myself first. It was important to remove the clouds hanging over me so I could learn to trust that God is leading me. And to be in His good graces, I could not live and love harboring the hurt of my past.

I've had a few hurts in my past, and while I was going through them, I felt like the pain would never end. Some hurts stemmed from failed relationships, marriage, and trouble with a business associate, whom, to this day, I have no confirmation as to why she stopped talking to me. I was hurt and disappointed but all I could think of during those times was to be vindictive in the marriage and relationships. I couldn't allow them to do better than I was doing. I lashed out at times and then bottled up my emotions without finalizing the pain. I did, however, move forward and live. But was I completely living if I was still unable to forgive?

I thought I was in love and everything was good but, as it turns out, I had no clue what my love and life would entail. I made bad decisions that caused me to get hurt in the process of learning how to love. That first pain of deceit and lies made me angry and resentful. Keep in mind, this was before I really knew God and had a relationship with Him. I just wanted to get even and, in doing so, I made more bad decisions and choices that affected me negatively. Anger and bitterness can lead you down the path of self-destruction, and you ultimately hurt only yourself. But I wasn't thinking about forgiveness.

After a breakup, I never allowed myself the time I needed to take full advantage of opportunities that were set in place for me; so again, I made decisions without totally seeing past the present. I moved on because I was young and free to decide what was best for me and, at that time, I wasn't thinking of how selfish I was being. I was living my life my way: Moving on from the hurt meant freedom from the pain.

It's a little embarrassing that it took three major breaks in my life for the light to come on and shine brightly in my face. When I took the time to stop and look in the mirror, admit my fault in this cycle, and turn to the ultimate forgiver, I could see clearly. God will prune us in our mess and, in His word, He promised to never leave us nor forsake us. In the midst of the mess, God is still there, waiting for us to make a shift and turn to Him.

I believe I have always been compelled to write. On all of the occasions in which I should've forgiven someone, I instead put the hurt into writing, in the form of a letter or some journal notes. At that time, I was compelled to write down my feelings so I wouldn't miss anything that was necessary for me to say. When people treat you badly and hurt you for no reason, it is our duty to forgive so that God may work in our favor. God was already there, preparing me for what was to be my future. I had to be equipped with the ability to forgive because He knew there were going to be some more challenges coming into my life.

The key to true forgiveness is first forgiving ourselves and, most times, we are the last to see we should have been forgiven first. In order to serve a living God, we must be cleansed from the filth of sin and shame (Psalm 103:12). When we truly ask God for forgiveness, He does just that and He is finished with it. We tend to ask for forgiveness and hold on to that which we have been forgiven; learn through prayer to let it go so God can work in your life.

If your heart is to be free, you must forgive anyone that has done wrong to you and, when you are guilty of doing harm to someone, always ask for forgiveness so you can live and not just exist. Do not allow bitterness to come between you and God. God has made it possible for you to know Him and experience an amazing change in your own life. Discover how you can find peace with God through the power of forgiveness.

Now, your resentment may be justified. The person may have done an evil, terrible thing to you. You may have every legal and intellectual right to hold a grudge and hate that person. But if you want to see miracles in your life, it is absolutely imperative that you forgive.

I know from my own experiences that it is not easy, letting go of past resentments, hurts, and pain. I myself was never very quick to forgive anyone who hurt me, and in the process, I was only hurting myself and hindering my blessings. I had to make up my mind to truly forgive in order to move on from the pain of the lost relationships and lost friendships to my ability to live and love completely. I recognized that, if I am going to be worthy of His blessings, then I must do as the Word tells us: We must forgive. It isn't an option; it is absolutely necessary to forgive your brothers and sisters, and, often times, they have to be forgiven more than once.

Now, forgiveness does not mean we condone, forget, or excuse a wrongful action or the hurt that ensued. Neither does it mean we must reconcile with the ones who wronged us. Instead, when we choose to forgive, we acknowledge what happened was wrong, we regain power, and we free ourselves from bondage. After all, God said in His word that He would fight our battles. Forgiveness releases the power of love in the form of acceptance, which allows the heart, mind, and body to function at its fullest potential. When we refuse to let go and forgive, our true selves become hidden or masked by our fear of yet another rejection, making us to appear emotionally non-existent to others, yet allowing them to continue to be in charge of your power. Hating or resenting, as explained by American existential psychologist Rollo May, is a superficial way of soothing our pain and preserving our sense of personal power and dignity; it ultimately gives away our power instead of declaring, "You have conquered me, but I reserve the right to hate you. We have the right to forgive so we can heal and live. God controls it all not us." Release any resentment and take back your power. If you do not, the pain you hold on to will always be a reminder, not only of your wounds and the person who wounded you, but also of the true need of healing.

We are human, therefore, deep down we have the desire to get empathy from the people who hurt us. You also may want them to openly admit the harm they caused. Cultural conditioning has impaired most of us to believe that fear and force, rather than love and choice, weigh heavy in getting our needs met or letting others know of our disappointments. Many of us don't practice peaceful resolution. We often times feel that aggression will help with the healing process, when actually, you are giving away your power, which is most definitely not an effective road to a healing a relationship. We must take full responsibility of restoring our own ability to heal and love.

Besides, many times, people are so focused on themselves and the path to your destruction that they are not going to have a true change of heart or care if they hurt or offended you. Forgiveness does not depend on whether the other person changes his or her ways, feels remorse, or even wants you to forgive. By imposing those conditions, you hand your power over to the one who acted wrongfully toward you.

You forgive for you, not for the sake of someone else. We may prefer others to ask for forgiveness and that they acknowledge the harm of what they did or did not do. We do not need this, however, to be happy and free to love. God can and will change things and hearts for there is nothing impossible with Him. As a result of coming to deeply see, feel, and recognize the pain they caused, your offenders may eventually come to ask for forgiveness and try to make things right. If it is truly of God, you have not given away your power. You have the power to let it go.

Letting go of bitterness is a gift you give to free yourself and move closer to God. You forgive to heal yourself, to restore the emotional power you need to remain empathically connected to your inner sense of compassion. You forgive to know yourself. Without a love-connection to yourself, you cannot connect with others. You forgive to honor your inner design, because love is the essence of who we are as human beings. Only God has the power to absolve anyone so learn to let go and let God. You love, live, and forgive because it is who you ultimately are, and therefore, in the highest interest of your health and well-being, forgive. In other words, you forgive to experience the fullness of your capacity to give and receive love.

The good news is that letting go of bitterness becomes easier with practice. Eventually, you will get to the point where, when someone does something hurtful to you, God is so prominent in your life that you will offer forgiveness to avoid the harmful, toxic life ahead by not choosing to forgive. Don't let resentment and lack of forgiveness stifle the greatness that is divinely in store for you. Are you willing to waste precious time and energy that can hinder your growth, harm your health, and block the blessing of newness in your next journeys?

There is action and reaction in forgiveness. We have to seek God in order for us to adjust to the positives ahead. Genuine forgiveness is a painful undertaking that consists of action, not a mere exchange of words such as "Would you forgive me?" and "Yes, I forgive you." As with genuine love, it is expressed in consistent action with conscious intention to do what is necessary to end needless suffering for yourself and other people. Remind yourself of this to create nourishing relationships and grow to love more courageously from a place of greater compassion and authenticity.

Ultimately, the power of forgiveness is fully accepting that something we never expected or wanted, even feared and tried desperately to avoid, has happened. All that means is simply that the event or offense is now over. It's in the past. Therefore, by dealing with a past disappointment with total acceptance, we are giving a gift of healing to our mind, body, and soul. Especially if the injury is ongoing or the wrongdoer won't or cannot take ownership of their offenses, the power of acceptance will free you to have total connection to your inner being. We always have a choice, and accepting that we cannot alter the past or another person allows us to own the power we have within us to change the ways we respond to and think about certain stimuli. Protecting our own happiness is our responsibility!

To forgive also allows you to consciously use your powers of imagination, choice, and creativity. It allows you to imagine the best possible future for yourself, one that requires you to perform a challenging task: To refuse pain, fear, or hurt to be the final word in your life. It's a challenge that calls you to give up life and relationship-harming thoughts and judgments about the other person, and instead, consciously formulate relationship-strengthening ones that allow you to stay connected to your infinite capacity for compassion, wisdom, and understanding. By learning to transform your experiences of pain, you turn losses into assets, and you destroy lies and illusions in which fear seems larger than life. The blessings have room to enter and grow to the fullest. The manifestation is real and evident in everything you do, once you decide to forgive, let go, and move on.

We can make a choice to forgive and an even greater choice to forget what others have done to hurt us. Remember that neither of these choices makes you weak. A strong person learns through the process to take the high road. Weak people don't know how to forgive, therefore, they hold on to the false sense of victory even when, in reality, they are defeated. God is true love and you can't have love or win unless you choose God's love. Forgiveness is a statement you make to yourself and others that says you choose to stay connected to your source and that you understand both the wondrous strengths and vulnerabilities we share. It says that you recognize this journey of life we are on is meant to stretch our limits and help us obtain stronger compassion towards one another so that we may individually realize our emotional fulfillment.

When I truly learned how to forgive myself, accept, let go, and move forward, I was released from the bondage of my past and, in that release, I took back my power. God blessed me with true friends who genuinely love me, a wonderful relationship/marriage, and new business partnerships. I'm free to live and love completely. Now, when I'm faced with opposition, I'm equipped with everything I need to move on. I protect my total body and never give myself away.

With that being said, forgiveness is something we may need to do again and again. But fear not: Love has no limits unless we place limits on ourselves. Let your wisdom guide your choices. Think about the consequences of not forgiving versus the results of forgiving, the risks of bitterness versus the benefits of acceptance, the misery of living in resentment versus living free to love. Think about the potential dangers of losing control of your behaviors to vindictive thinking versus a life in which compassion is a guiding force to help you love and live your best life. The choice is yours. Learn to forgive so that no one takes away your power to love. Learn to let go so you can live powerfully. Forgive as God requests, so He can forgive you.

Take back your power. Let it go and move on.

> "For if you forgive men when they sin against you, your heavenly Father will also forgive you. But if you do not forgive men their sins, your Father will not forgive your sins."
>
> —Matthew 6:14-15

> "Then Peter came to Jesus and asked, 'Lord, how many times shall I forgive my brother when he sins against me? Up to seven times?' Jesus answered, 'I tell you, not seven times, but seventy-seven times. Therefore, the kingdom of heaven is like a king who wanted to settle accounts with his servants. As he began the settlement, a man who owed him ten thousand talents was brought to him. Since he was not able to pay, the master ordered that he and his wife and his children and all that he had be sold to repay the debt.'"
>
> —Matthew 18:21-25

> "If we really want to love, we must learn how to forgive."
>
> —Mother Theresa

God Blessed Me with the Desire of My Heart...Now What?

ALEXANDRIA L. BARLOWE

My body instantly tensed and tightened as they wheeled me into the operating room. It felt like a refrigerator in there.

"You're going to die," I heard a voice say. "You're not going to make it out of this room alive and neither will she."

It was the enemy. Too often, I let him defeat me with a barrage of negative thoughts. But no more. After what took place on that day in that operating room, God began to unravel a chain of events that taught me to overcome. He would provide a way for me to learn to quiet that oppressive voice for good.

Of course, I didn't know any of this when I was in the operating room. "Why does it have to be so cold in here?" I wondered, and shivered as the anesthesiologist explained the medication she was about to administer. She told me that I would feel the lower half of my body go cold. She also told me that she would make sure I was properly numbed before the doctor began surgery. As she instructed me to hold still and gently bend my back towards her, I began to shiver violently and a cloak of terror overcame me. I began to cry. I had never been more afraid than I was in that moment.

What if it hurts so bad I jump? I couldn't breathe, let alone hold still.

"This is going to hurt. It is going to hurt a lot," the voice said again. "You're going to move and the needle is going to pierce your spinal nerve. You're going to be paralyzed."

The nurse sensed my fear and comforted me. "Sweetheart, don't be afraid," she said warmly as she rubbed my arm and embraced me. "You've got this. You can do this. I'm right here with you. I'm going to help you through this."

She gave me a pillow helped me get into the proper position. She held my hand and her words were like the warm blanket that I so desperately needed in that freezing cold room. The terror subsided and my body relaxed. I breathed deeply, followed the anesthesiologist's instructions, and gently pushed my back towards her while holding on to the pillow. To my surprise, the needle was not that bad; the fear of it was far worse than the momentary pin-prick. I realized that the fear of the unknown had reared its head in that moment.

Can you relate? Have you ever experienced something that was not as bad as you thought it was? Have you ever prepared for the worst only to find that the worst never came to pass? Chances are, you answered "yes" to one of those questions—so you feel my pain, right?

Just as the anesthesiologist forewarned, I began to feel my legs go cold. "Could it get any colder in here?" I asked myself. I took deep breaths and tried to focus on something else. "I'm going to be okay," I told myself. "Everything is going to be just fine."

"Good morning, Alex! The big day is finally here. Can you believe it?"

Dr. Walker had such a bright and bubbly voice. I had come to adore her in the prior weeks. My favorite thing about her is that she is a believer too.

"I'm as ready as I'm going to get," I responded.

"Well, let's all gather, hold hands, and pray," she said.

I was so relieved and thanked God for this praying doctor. In that moment, God knew I was afraid of entering these unchartered waters. He knew that He needed to show me that He had everything under control. His answer could not have been more clear than my doctor leading us in prayer before surgery.

"God, I ask that You guide my hands this morning," she prayed. "I thank You in advance for a smooth procedure with no incident or complications. In Your name we pray, Amen."

After the prayer, Dr. Walker scrubbed in and prepared to perform the surgery that would change my life forever. Next, the anesthesiologist explained that I would feel a pressure but not pain. She said that, if at any time I felt pain, I should let her know immediately so that she could increase the numbing medication. Would you agree that God want us to do the same? He wants us to let Him know when we feel pain so that He can administer the healing we need. I calmed down as I felt God with me throughout this entire spiritual experience.

With fear subsided, I was able to take it all in. "I can't believe this," I thought to myself. "The day and moment is finally here. I've been waiting for this day my whole life and now it is finally here." I began to cry tears of joy. What an emotional roller coaster! At first I was crying because I was petrified, and now I was crying because I was overjoyed. The nurse told me that she would go and get my husband.

James was cool, calm, and collected as he entered the operating room. Seeing him immediately put me at ease and reminded me that I was not in this alone. I realized that the scariest part of this day was now over and it was now the moment we had all been waiting for.

"You okay?" He asked.

"Yes, I'm okay, honey. Are you?"

"Yeah, I'm fine if you're fine," he said. "It's so cold in here."

"I know!" I said and laughed.

He looked around and saw all of the tools and equipment. He didn't say much but I could tell that he was taking it all in. He sat looking at everything and at me.

"Your hand goes here," one of the nurses said, grabbing his hand and placing it in mine.

"My bad," he said, laughing. He held my hand and the nurse asked if he wanted to see the surgery take place. "No, thank you," he said. We had just talked the night before about how he can't stand the sight of blood.

"Do you want me to take pictures?" the nurse asked.

I said yes because I wanted to see as much as I could. My doctor explained that I would feel lots of pulling and tugging, a lot of pressure.

"It's going to feel like an elephant is sitting on your chest," she explained. "This is normal so don't be alarmed. Remember, it will be pressure, not pain."

Just as she explained, I felt that pressure. "Wow," I said, trying to breathe deeply.

"Are you okay?" James asked.

"Yes, I'm fine," I replied.

Indeed, I felt that elephant sitting on my chest. It was insurmountable. I had never experienced so much pressure. Isn't it funny how pressure creates diamonds or pressure cooks the chicken? In this moment, I had a true understanding of all of these facts. I was experiencing the greatest physical pressure of my life. I was also experiencing the greatest mental and emotional pressure of my life: Pressure to be the best mother to this beautiful child who God blessed us with. Pressure to make sure that she has everything that she needs. Pressure to raise her to be an upstanding individual with a good head on her shoulders. Motherhood was a new frontier for me and I had never felt a greater responsibility than I did in this moment. In the birth of my daughter, I knew that God was my soul source. I knew that there was no way I could mother this little person without His help. Every moment before this one seemed so small now.

As the tugging and pulling continued, I took more deep breaths.

"You alright?" James asked again.

A tear leaked out of my eye. The same nurse who put his hand in mine just moments before gave him a tissue and he wiped my tears. After about ten minutes of pulling and tugging and that insane pressure on my chest, I heard her crying. That was my baby girl. I couldn't believe it. So many months of anticipation had finally come to fruition.

James saw her before I did. "She's got a head full of hair," he said excitedly.

The nurse lifted her up over the cover so that I could see her. Words can't describe how I felt to see my baby girl in the flesh. Her little face was scrunched up. Her little eyes were puffy and still closed. That was my Vivian; all five pounds, five ounces, and eighteen inches of her. She was a tiny little thing and my heart skipped a beat the moment I first saw her. I watched in awe as the nurse cleaned her up and swaddled her. James stood watching the nurse, staring at this little person who we had been anxiously waiting to meet for the last thirty-seven weeks. I could tell what he was thinking: "Oh my God, that is my daughter." When the nurse finished, she let James hold her. Vivian immediately grabbed his finger. The nurse was kind enough to snap a picture of her tiny pale little hand grasping onto her daddy's ginormous finger.

The following few days in the hospital were rough to say the least. I was groggy and on pain medication while struggling to nurse. A lactation consultant said that nursing was of the utmost importance because she was so small.

"Most babies lose weight within their first twenty-four hours after delivery," she said bluntly. "She could weigh four pounds by the end of the evening."

The problem was that Vivian was about three weeks early so my milk supply hadn't come in yet. I tried pumping as much as I possibly could but only got a couple of drops of colostrum. In those trying hours, I knew I had to rely solely on God to help me and to give my baby girl the strength to grow healthy and strong. Sure enough, I kept my sweetie on a rigorous feeding schedule and she never dipped below five pounds. Today, she is a precocious and happy seven-month-old, weighing in at fifteen pounds and measuring twenty-five inches long.

Vivian is the greatest thing that has ever happened to me. I fall more in love with her each and every day. I can't get enough of the wonderment that fills her big, beautiful, brown eyes every time she sees something new. I never get tired of her giddy laugh, complete with her tongue hanging out. I laugh hysterically at her little gummy grin that is currently adorned with two tiny teeth on the bottom. Most of all, I love cuddling with her when she is fighting her sleep or watching her play with her favorite toy, Mr. Ducky. James is absolutely smitten with her as well. I've never seen him look at anyone the way he looks at her. His face lights up when he comes home from work and greets her with a big hug and tickle match. I love it when he tries to put her to sleep but ends up putting himself to sleep as well.

In this chapter of my life, I can honestly say that God has given me beauty for ashes. This time five years ago, I was depressed, lonely, and contemplating suicide because of the end of my first marriage. After signing the divorce papers, I swore that I would never love again, let alone marry again. Then six months later, I married James, packed up as much as I could fit in the trunk of his Dodge Charger, and left my hometown for Dallas. I remember all of the ups and downs that I went through to get to this point. I remember praying for the things I have now and I am careful to thank God each and every day. I realize now that all of the heartache and pain were simply parts of my process. If I had not endured those dark days, I would not appreciate the sunshine in my life as much as I do now.

So, when did I confirm that God is my sole source and my soul's only source? When He finally blessed me with the desire of my heart: A family. You see, in order to be a good steward of this blessing, I had to and continue to rely on Him each and every day. I had to rely solely on him in order to fight through the hormonal rollercoasters that came with postpartum depression. I had to rely solely on him to deal with the excruciating incision pain from my C-section. I had to rely solely on him to survive the sleepless nights of the oh-so-trying first few weeks with a newborn. I had to rely solely on him to help me through the struggles of low milk supply and painful breastfeeding. Most of all, I had to rely solely on him to help me cope with the newfound anxiety that came about with my responsibilities as a mom. Am I doing this right? Is she going to get sick? Is she eating enough? These thoughts raced through my mind constantly in my first few months of motherhood. With every new phase of Vivian's growth and development, there are new milestones for her to meet and new things for me to incorporate into her daily routine. I take my role as a mother very seriously and I am dedicated to being the best mom I can be. To have the patience, wisdom, and strength it takes to raise a child, I must rely solely on Him.

I must also rely solely on God to be the best wife that I can be. With five years of marriage under my belt, I have learned that this is always easier said than done. I have to rely solely on God to ensure that I am always considerate of my husband in everything that I do and say. I have to rely solely on God to ensure that I reciprocate the love and dedication that he shows me each and every day. I have to rely solely on God to make sure that I am not only my husband's lover but also his friend. Although marriage is a beautiful thing, it is certainly not rainbows and romance every day. It is in those taxing times that I have learned that I must rely solely on God. I have learned that He didn't give me the desires of my heart for me to be careless with them or to take them for granted. He predestined me to be James' wife and Vivian's mother for a purpose.

I want to close by asking you a question: What chapter are you currently in in your life? Are you in a period of darkness? Does everything around you seem to be falling apart no matter how hard you try? Are you in a phase of your life in which God has given you beauty for ashes? Regardless of where you are right now, you must realize that God is your soul's only source! Even if you feel like everything in your life is going beautifully and happening as planned...you still need God! You need Him to help you walk in His purpose for your life. If you are currently experiencing a season of darkness, you most certainly must understand that God is your soul's only source and only way out of the darkness. I know and completely understand what it is like to not want to live anymore. I know what it's like to have absolutely no faith. I know what it's like to question God's every move and doubt His presence in your life. I know because I have been there, and because I have been there, I can tell you two things.

First, it gets better! I promise it does. After I married James in 2012, I wrote a book chronicling my life story and personal testimony. James came up with the title, *No Good Thing*, which is based on Psalm 84:11: "For the Lord God is a sun and shield. The Lord will give grace and glory. No good thing will he withhold from them that walk uprightly." Second and last, I said it once and I am going to say it again: God is your sole source! His love and comfort will guide you through your life.

I want you to know that I am praying with and for you. You are not alone and you are loved. God called you and graced you to endure this time you are in. I know it doesn't always feel good, but trust me: There is beauty on the other side. There is peace and joy. There is laughter so deep that you won't even remember the countless tears you've cried. If you remember nothing else from my story, please remember that God is your sole source and your soul's one true source for everything that you need.

It Starts With Me

DEANDRA D. PRITCHETT

"May the God of hope fill you with all joy and peace as you trust in him, so that you may overflow with hope by the power of the Holy Spirit."

—Romans 15:13 (NIV)

"A journey of a thousand miles begins with a single step."

—Lao Tzu

I was born in Gary, Indiana as the oldest of eight children. We were the family who seemed to be at church whenever the doors opened. Sunday service, weekly Bible studies, practices and revival—all of it. My dad was known as the head deacon and one of the church musicians, while my mother and grandmother were highly respected women in our community. Despite the spiritual background that was exemplified in my family, there were many things that I did not understand in my younger years. This led to years of struggling with low self-esteem, insecurities, anger, and a bout with making poor decisions.

Today, as a wife, mom, and educator, I find myself backtracking my history in order to gain ground on who God has called Deandra Pritchett to be. I knew early on that I had the gift of gab and influence, but couldn't quite find my rhythm as God would have it. Can you relate? I hope so, because it is my desire and intention that each one of you who reads my story will begin to see the divine purpose and will that God has on your life. While God may not show you everything all at once, He sheds light on areas that suit your divine destination. It is up to each individual to take responsibility for how he or she responds to the circumstances (good or bad) in life, which happens when our hearts are open to the divine nature of change that comes through God. This very message allows us to see the transformational difference between an individual who will *thrive* in life versus one who will simply *exist*.

As a child, I was raised in a Pentecostal environment where there were plenty of strict policies and rules. Such rules included no colored nail polish, no pants, and no going to the movies. Although I was young, I paid very close attention to things that took place around me, so I was very aware that my parents did not see eye-to-eye on the various policies of our church. I never felt as if God would love anyone based on man-made rules. They are amazing parents, but this idea was conflicting for me. So, as I grew older into a teen, I rejected some of the church rules because I wanted to be myself (whatever that meant).

The problem with this decision was that, no matter what, there was always some sort of conflict going on in my mind. I didn't know if I was being rebellious or just distrustful of what I learned in church. I began searching for what "felt" right for me. Regardless of my background, I never stopped to consider the foundation that was put in place for me to function as the young lady God created me to be. I took it for granted. Honestly, I took God for granted. I went with the notion of "once saved, always saved" without actively doing my part.

What does it mean to do your part? Well, first of all, Colossians 1:10 (NASB) says, "so that you may live a life worthy of the Lord and please him in every way: bearing fruit in every good work, growing in the knowledge of God." Simply put, we are called to consider the ways of God in everything that we do. This includes how we treat others, how we act or behave in and out of the public eye, as well as how we manage our time. This also means spending intentional time with God and embracing His word for ourselves. This happens when we truly take heed of what the Holy Spirit is saying to us and through us.

So, I spent a great amount of my teen years *not* doing my part. Since I was on a journey of searching for what I "felt" was right, I fell for many things that were no good for me. I lost my virginity at the age of fifteen, partied with the wrong crowd, and slept around with guys who meant me no good. Many of those felt like out-of-body experiences. I really believe that, in my own way, I was crying out for help, but didn't slow down long enough to receive the help that was right in front of me. However, I can truly say that God never left my side. There were moments in which I felt His presence amidst my sin. I knew and understood that, while He did not condone all of my actions, God had His hand on my life.

When I was eighteen and had graduated from high school, I met an older guy who seemed to be the sweetest and most gentle man ever. We began to spend a lot of time together. However, the more I would converse with him, the more uncomfortable I felt. I never counted that unction or feeling as the Holy Spirit until later. Despite my sexual past, I was very adamant about just going out to dinner or having candid conversations with him over the phone, without having sex with him. Did he question it? Yes. Did I consider it? Yes.

As time went on, we became distant and eventually lost touch with each other. Six months later, a friend told me that he was diagnosed with the AIDS virus. I wept for hours because I knew that it was only by the grace of God that I was able to walk away from all those sexual encounter without contracting that deadly virus. I had never felt so connected to God until that moment. He was there, despite the unwise decisions that I'd made in the past. Romans 3:21-24 (ESV) says, "But now the righteousness of God has been manifested apart from the law, although the Law and the Prophets bear witness to it— the righteousness of God through faith in Jesus Christ for all who believe. For there is no distinction: for all have sinned and fall short of the glory of God, and are justified by his grace as a gift, through the redemption that is in Christ Jesus."

While we have to do our part of showing God that we can be disciplined and loving individuals who boldly walk by faith, God's grace is not dependent on any of those things. I understood that God loved me. I also believed that He had great things in store for my life. However, I could not firmly grasp what that required of me. So, I started placing a greater focus on serving at church and spending time with the older women at the church, because I wanted to show God that I appreciated who He was in my life. I also had a desire to be a more mature young lady.

But despite my efforts, I eventually drifted away from serving and going to church because I still felt as if I was being judged and not encouraged along the way. Soon after I turned twenty-one, I met my husband, who, at the time, was just someone whom I met and slept with. Well, in a matter of weeks, I became pregnant. I was shocked and embarrassed all at the same time. I felt as if God was trying to slow me down. Well, He did just that!

As a young adult, now pregnant with my first child, I was forced to become less self-absorbed and more focused on making responsible decisions that would positively impact my life as well as my daughter's. So, despite my having a very casual relationship with the father of my child, I prayed for our relationship to flourish into something more than just sex. Thanks to God's plan for my life along with the sincerity of my heart, my prayer was answered. At the time, I did not fully understand how my life would be impacted, but I knew that I wanted more. It started with my understanding that God had to be the central focus.

Does that mean that my husband and I immediately lived happily after? Definitely not! Over the years, we have definitely experienced many highs and lows in our marriage, but God has been so faithful every step of the way. In the beginning, just as most couples are, we were so in love and excited about our new journey together. However, that *feeling* of excitement and love started to dwindle. As a new wife, all of my habits that existed prior to marriage began to make their way into our home, including any pre-conceived notions about how I believed a husband or father should be. I would even go as far as telling my husband that he needed to be like other husbands that were in our lives. This was difficult for my husband, but it was also for me—I thought for many years that, if God was gracious enough to bless me with the marriage that I prayed for, then surely my husband would function according to how I thought he should in order for me to be "happy." Was I wrong or what?

Instead of trusting God to make the necessary changes in our lives, I decided to take matters into my own hands. I began to feel as though I was entitled to have what I thought I should have, including the type of house I wanted and my favorite car, as well as how my husband should treat me in front of his family and mine. However, what I did not grasp was that God was trying to do something contrary to my plans, and He made it obvious: Nothing ever fell into place like I wanted it to. Instead, things always led to strife and division. Still, I would feel so justified that I would not have a care or concern about who witnessed me arguing with my husband. I could not see past my own expectations, hopes, and dreams for my marriage, and I saw pride play an impactful, but negative role in my life. Despite this, God had ways of getting my attention while showering His love on my family and me.

In 2008, when the housing market took a hit, we were one of the families that lost our home to foreclosure. This was devastating, embarrassing, and a little scary at times. Our family spent months and years shifting from one place to the next in rental homes, as well as living with church and family members. To be honest, we couldn't be frustrated with anyone but ourselves; but at the same time, we knew that we needed the hand of God to lead and guide us to make effective and life-changing decisions. It just seemed like, every time we thought we were making progress, something else would happen and push us back further than where we started.

Things became more intense when we found ourselves homeless. With little money in hand, we had nowhere to go for six months. Instead of basking in the frustrations of the matter, my husband and I began to pray and ask for guidance. Then, we made a list of the things that we hoped God would manifest during this time. As we continued to pray and form a bond of unity, God moved on our behalf: He showed us favor in our jobs, church, and with individuals who we'd never even met before. He also blessed us with a place to call home. I Corinthians 1:9 (ESV) says, "God is faithful, by whom you were called into the fellowship of his Son, Jesus Christ our Lord." Our hope was intensified when He showed us who our true source is on earth.

There were many times when I would acknowledge the direction of the Holy Spirit, while other times, I would take heed of my own feelings and actions. Nevertheless, I would slowly see how God orchestrated different situations in our lives. He would show me just enough to let me know that He is still in control. Despite all of that, I was still not disciplined enough to not allow my emotions to rule my life.

There was a time when everything in my marriage had hit rock bottom. I had become so angry, bitter, and disgusted with all that had taken place that I could not see a way out. This time, we considered divorce. I remember feeling every negative emotion all at the same time. I literally felt paralyzed by those very feelings that overwhelmed my heart and mind.

Then, during one heated debate with my husband, there was a moment in our conversation when I had to make a decision to either go with pride or to surrender. As much as my flesh wanted to fight for my rights and feelings, I could not take it anymore. I was tired of going through the emotional roller coasters. I was fed up with the enemy playing games with my life. I was frustrated with not living with the joy that God gave each and every one of us. After all, how can I expect for God to make an example out of me if I am not walking out His will? My overall posture began to bow before God.

I started reflecting on the passage in II Corinthians 5:17(KJV), " Therefore if any man *be* in Christ, *he is* a new creature: old things are passed away; behold, all things are become new." I began to focus my mind on doing things that exemplified the love of Christ. I began to pray for my husband more often and to pray for my influence within our home. I also decided not to allow my mistakes to distract me. I am not perfect, but I am made whole in Christ Jesus. So, I was laser-focused on ending this journey well instead of being overwhelmed by how it started.

Let's consider that for a moment: How many times have you been so inundated with your mistakes and past failures that it caused you to de-value where God has you right now? When we carry on in that manner, our vision becomes blurred. That's to say that the plan and vision of God is there, but you are out of focus because you are wearing the wrong lens. You have to remove the lens of selfishness, doubt, pride, and anything that reflects your past. This can only be done with the help of God, your one and only true source.

There is nothing like allowing God to be the center of your life. This means that I no longer had to or would live a life of condemnation about my past. No matter how many times I messed up, His love carried me through it all. I am not my mistakes. You are not your mistakes. When I intentionally began to rely on His wisdom, direction, and peace, things became clear for me to see. True progress can never take place if we are too prideful to receive correction. Real success will never be attained when we are too stubborn to pursue transparency with God. Yes, He knows all, but it makes a difference when we are open about our own shortcomings. I encourage you to take off the blinders and receive the gift of the Holy Spirit in your life. John 14:26 says, "But the Advocate, the Holy Spirit, whom the Father will send in my name, will teach you all things and will remind you of everything I have said to you." Many people are searching for tips, tricks, and words of motivation for their life. The Holy Spirit can and will provide all of that to those that will take heed to His direction. Are you willing?

This requires you to humble yourself while allowing the truth of God to break down any barriers that serve as stumbling blocks. You are not alone. There were many times when I cried out to God about my hurt, pain, shame, and disgust with myself and others. Afterwards, I would have a good ugly cry, and the peace of God would consume my mind, heart, and overall emotions. I don't know about you, but I want to live in the true abundance of God. No exceptions!

I have spent too many years trying to live my way. Well, guess what? That was not good enough for me to function as a wife, mother, daughter, sister, teacher, speaker, and entrepreneur. I can tell you that, today, I am intentionally living for God. I am intentionally trusting in Him because He is my one true source. It started with me confessing my sins to

God. It started with me submitting my will to Him. It started with me declaring greatness over my life.

You can do the same. Look in the mirror and say: It starts with me!

Out of Darkness and Into the Light

YOLANDA WILLIAMS

"For I am convinced that neither death nor life, neither angels nor demons, neither the present nor the future, nor any powers, neither height nor depth, nor anything else in all creation, will be able to separate us from the love of God that is in Christ Jesus our Lord."

—Romans 8:38-39(NIV)

"Even the darkest night will end and the sun will rise."

—Victor Hugo

To cheer means to encourage, congratulate, and applaud one to victory. It means to inspire or incite excitement and enthusiasm to triumph. That's who I am: The person who tells you you're going to make it when you are on your last leg. The person who tells you not to quit when you don't know if you're making a difference. The person who supports your big goal when you don't believe you can accomplish it. The person who encourages you, pushes you to keep going, and applauds for the victory you can't see. The person who, no matter what you say or believe, will remind you that God has given you everything you need to be victorious. That is who I am.

Yes, my role as a pastor requires a certain skill set, but it's more than checking off boxes of required traits. Encouraging, praising, and inspiring people to victory as easily as you breathe comes from the inside. I know that's exactly who God created me to be. It's a part of my DNA.

> *"For you created my inmost being; you knit me together in my mother's womb. I praise you because I am fearfully and wonderfully made; your works are wonderful."*
>
> *—Psalm 139: 13-14*

Although it sounds nice now, I, at first, didn't want to accept the fact that I was the cheerleader. I really wanted to change people's perception of me. In my opinion, cheerleaders had no substance. I was not the go-getter, the one to make it happen. I was not the planning guru or the financial wizard. I was not the one people came to for spiritual advice, even though I was a pastor. I was the cheerleader. That's it. The cheerleader.

Now, I know what I felt was based on stereotypes. In actuality, I know that cheerleaders are trained athletes, skilled gymnasts, and dancers whose very presence can motivate and encourage a crowd and lead a team to victory. Nonetheless, the idea of being known as the cheerleader did not sit well with me. I didn't feel validated because I knew I *was* a go-getter and a planning guru. I *did* give sound spiritual advice. And yet, when people described me, I was only the cheerleader. I didn't feel like I added anything to the team. I didn't see God's works as wonderful, nor did I believe that I was fearfully and wonderfully made.

It's a trick of the enemy to make you see yourself other than how God sees you. Instead of seeing God's wonderful creation, you feel less than, not good enough, not worthy. Let me tell you: He did not make a mistake when He created you. He put characteristics in you that are unique! The way you walk, your laugh, your personality, what moves you, the way you move—all of it. There is no one like you, and your life makes a difference in someone else's life. On days you can't seem to see who God sees, tell yourself, "I am fearfully and wonderfully made. I am chosen, holy, and blameless before God. He is my source and He doesn't make mistakes." Once you say it, walk in it.

> *"Train up a child in the way he should go, And when he is old he will not depart from it."*
> —Proverbs 22:6 (NKJV)

I grew up in church. I sang in the youth choir, played the piano for the Sunday School, planned activities for the youth department, and attended every program and revival the church had. Simply put, if the church had it, I was there. I knew God, but only as God of church, not of my life. It wasn't until my sophomore year in college at a gospel concert (I sang in the choir) that I accepted Him as my personal Savior and really understood what that meant.

But I did say it happened in college, and trust me: I fully experienced college life! I was sure of my salvation, but my walk...well, that was different. Two years after I graduated, I got married and moved to California, the place where dreams are made. Subconsciously, I saw living in California as a sign of success. My life looked picture perfect and I was doing all the right things. After all, both my husband and I had corporate jobs we loved, we hung out with friends, and we were involved in a church we loved. I was studying His word and connecting with other people who walked with God. What I realized later was that my spiritual growth was intellectual at best, and while that's good, there is something different about knowing beyond a shadow of a doubt where your help comes from. I knew and loved God, but God wasn't personal.

Time went on and my marriage went through the ups and downs typical of any marriage. We were high school sweethearts and had had a long-distance relationship before we married. We had unrealistic expectations of each other and it wasn't working. We knew who we remembered each other to be in high school and that wasn't reconciling with who we were as adults. And because we didn't know each other, everything about marriage was hard. Nonetheless, we weathered those early marital storms, as well as his lay-off from the job he loved and the deaths of his father, my grandmother, and my grandfather.

I got pregnant and gave birth to an amazing daughter followed by the birth of an equally amazing son. After the second pregnancy, I truly was under the impression that I was superwoman. I had my son in September, went back to work in November, took a four-year-old and a three-month-old across the country, celebrated the holidays with my family in December, and began work on a congressional political campaign in January. You know the superwoman syndrome—you believe you can do it all.

Anybody else could see it was all too much, but often, others will see what we refuse to see. For me, I was just doing what I do. I love to be involved, and my gifts of administration and leadership lend greatly to my involvement on planning committees of all interests. However, my need to be a part of something big was far more important than my need for self-preservation. Before I knew it, I was exhausted—not just tired, but operating in sheer exhaustion. Raising two children and working full-time on a campaign while keeping my full-time job never struck me as odd. Looking back, I have to admit that doing all of that was absolutely insane! I have since learned to say no and not feel guilty. "No" is one of the best words in the English language!

I also learned that nothing is as important as your health. God had to help me with that lesson. As only He can, He orchestrated a three-month leave of absence from my job. This was something that only God could have done because I would not have had the foresight to even imagine that as a possibility. As a matter of fact, I argued with God about the timing of the leave, about the request, about everything! My desk was piled high with work, my assistant had just resigned, and I needed to help plan a leadership retreat. How dare He tell me to take a three-month leave?! Some people would've welcomed the break but I saw it as a sign of weakness. How would this look? How can I ask my boss to do this? Did He realize how unfair this was?

Even as I cried, I knew I would be obedient. I would do what He told me to do and would ask for the three-month leave of absence with pay. At the time, I worked as a director of human resources for a national staffing firm and the owner was a believer. She did not flinch when I told her what I had to do. Instead, she simply said, "If that's what He told you, then let's do it."

So, I took a leave of absence. I rested. I spent quality time with my husband and children, and I read my Word and prayed. My relationship with the Lord grew; but even as I said He was Lord of my life, I now realize that I was still operating in my own strength. I did and said all the things you were supposed to do and say. But I just knew that, once I rested and re-grouped, I would be ready to take on the world and go back to running my life.

Three months later, I put my son in day-care and went back to work. Pretty soon, everything was back to "normal." Day care, school, work, activities, church—the routine started all over again. I was reading the Word, I was praying, and I was involved in ministry. My life had become nothing more than just existing. I had no feelings of whether my life was good or bad; it just *was*. I was missing the joy in living and I just did what I had to do. During this time, I can't say God wasn't there because intellectually, I knew that He was. It was me who just existed. I stayed in that state for years.

> *Depression is a feeling of drowning while everyone else around you is breathing.*
> —Unknown

It came quietly before I even recognized it. One day it was light, and the next it was as if someone turned the lights off and I was in total darkness. Imagine the darkest, coldest place you can think of: There is no light. You can't see your hands in front of your face. You can't see anything—no shapes, no colors, no faces, nothing. You feel like you are at the bottom of a dark, cold pit, and there is no way out. You don't know whether to move forward, move backward, or just stand still. Now that you've pictured that, multiply that feeling by three. That was my life.

It was depression unlike anything I had ever experienced. I lived in total and complete darkness. Any light would have been good, but there was nothing. It was a struggle just to get out of bed even though I had to because I was a wife, I was a mother, I had a job, and I had to keep going. Staying in bed was not an option, though it was the only thing that made me happy.

I couldn't tell anybody what was happening. I was living a life that looked like all was well, a life that most people would say I should be thankful for. I was just tired, right? I would get over it, right? At least, that's what I thought people would say. So, I hid it. I smiled, I laughed, I hung out with friends, and I managed the school book fair.

During this time, I drove to Las Vegas with my brother and sister. We always pray a simple prayer before we get on the road, and this time, I was designated to pray. The prayer was more than a simple "protect us on the highway." It was "Help us, Lord, and give our lives meaning." It was a desperate prayer. When I was done praying, my brother looked at me and said, "Wow, I just thought we were going to Vegas. God is going to do all that in Vegas?" My despair was oozing out but I chose not to share what I was going through with my family.

"It's not the time," I rationalized. "They can't handle it."

So off to Vegas we went. We stayed at the Mandalay Bay Hotel, and although it was a beautiful day, I sat at the pool in total darkness with a smile plastered on my face. I'm told the pool at the Mandalay Bay is one of the best in Vegas and I can't even tell you what it looked like. Why was I feeling like this? What was happening to me? My life had no meaning, no purpose. Yes, I had a great husband, wonderful children, a good job, and family and friends who loved me, but that wasn't enough. My life had turned into something I didn't recognize and it left me feeling empty and hopeless.

After that trip, I got worse. I considered going to the doctor because maybe all I needed was medication, but I couldn't muster the energy to go. I did what I had to do and nothing more. I couldn't pray because I didn't know what to pray for or about. My emotions evolved from despair to anger. At this point, some of my close friends knew something was wrong. Whenever they would tell me they were praying for me, outwardly I would say, "Thank you," but inwardly, I would get angry. I didn't want to hear anything about what God was saying so I would go to church only when I had to. I would sit in the back and leave before the sermon. Some Sundays, I would take my daughter to children's church and sit in the parking lot until she was done. Little by little, day by day, I was dying inside. Who would understand the despair I was feeling? How did I get here and how come I couldn't shake it? Where was God in all of this?

"...because God has said, "Never will I leave you; never will I forsake you."

—Hebrews 13:5 (NIV)

When I think about my life and the lives of many women, I realize that most of us just exist. We do what we have to do to make it. We get up in the morning, get dressed, get the kids off to school, get the husband off to work, go to work, come home, make dinner, put the kids to bed, go to bed, and get up to do it all over again. Don't get me wrong—we are hanging out with friends, we are going out on dates, and we are laughing. Life, at least on the outside, looks good. But, often times, in reality, we are walking around in darkness. The more we try to hide it, the darker it gets. We believe we have to be all things and, in that, we lose who we are and whose we are.

After six months in the darkness, I was lying in bed, the only place where I found peace, and I cried out in anger. I yelled out, "Where are you? I can't keep going like this. I'm drowning. Show me what I need to do and I will do it. Just don't leave me like this!" I cried myself to sleep that night and when I woke up the next day—nothing. The day after that—nothing. The day after that—nothing. Five days after I broke down, I opened my eyes and there was light. In my darkness, I saw a speck of light.

Mind you, it was not a big, bright light. The light was the size of the tip of a ball-point pen. But it was enough to let me know God heard me! For the first time in months, I got out of bed with hope. Coming out of the darkness was a slow process, but I started to feel again. He put people in my life who encouraged me to journal, which I had done in the past but was inconsistent about. This time, I journaled consistently, which caused me to face some things about my life that were not pleasing to God; but I realized that, even while those bad attitudes and judgmental thoughts came up, He never left me.

Someone else told me about affirmations. I had heard about affirmations but I didn't put much stock in it. However, during this time, I was willing to try anything because I couldn't go back to the darkness. I affirmed who I was in Christ and that spoke to who He was in my life. The process out of my depression was hard and slow, but through it, I came to totally depend on God. He was my lifeline and I knew that, without Him, I could not make it. It was no longer about what I knew intellectually. It was about what I believed in my heart; it was personal.

> *"...weeping may endure for a night, but joy comes in the morning."*
> —Psalms 30:5 (NKJV)

It came quietly before I even recognized it. I can't say exactly when it happened but, one morning, I woke up and the sun was shining. I got out of bed smiling. The darkness was gone and I was walking in the light. My joy was back! I loved life again! I was living my life with enthusiasm and excitement, and I was encouraging everyone around me to do the same. I know that I would not have made it without God. As I plugged back into Him, He showed me that I was operating as if I could do all things without Him. I exhausted myself and was in darkness because I was my own source. Even though I was doing the "right" things, I was doing them in my own strength. I was being superwoman or trying to be superwoman without acknowledging where my help was coming from. It's not just in your big decisions or major life's moments that you need God, but in the everyday routines of your life. God is your power source. No matter the details of your life, God wants you to depend completely on Him. Plug into God's light!

When life overwhelms you and you feel like you're drowning:

- Tell somebody: I kept everything inside which was eating me up. You don't have to tell everybody (as a matter of fact, you shouldn't tell everybody), but you must tell somebody. It can be a therapist, a pastor, or a friend. Tell somebody you trust who can hold you up and help you keep your head above water.
- Write it down: By journaling, you unlock all the thoughts in your head. Journal what's happening in your life, your doubts, your fears, everything. It's for you, so it doesn't have to be perfect. Putting your insides on paper can give you a different perspective. When you go back and read your words, God shows it to you differently.
- Speak affirmations: Proverbs 18:21 says, "Death and life are in the power of the tongue." Speak life! It may feel awkward if you are not used to repeating affirmations, but just keep doing it. Remind yourself that you are victorious and there is nothing that you and God can't handle. The more you speak it, the more you believe it. The more you believe it, the more it becomes a part of your DNA.

Loss and Rejection: That Stuff Challenges Your Faith

REGINA M. POOLE

"Troubled on every side, yet not distressed; we are perplexed, but not in despair; Persecuted, but not forsaken; cast down, but not destroyed."
—2 Corinthians 4:8-9

"Go where you are celebrated, not where you are tolerated."
—Bishop Otis Lockett, Sr., Evangel Fellowship, Greensboro, NC

There are not many things in my life that have the ability to tear at my heart. I don't consider myself to be "soft." I prefer *The Godfather* to *The Notebook* and mixed martial arts to ice skating. I've watched *The Imitation of Life* and not shed a tear. I have very few shades of grey and I openly welcome confrontation. I am not necessarily emotional, but I am passionate. I don't share any of this to boast about how strong and emotionally resilient I am. This "feigned" strength and tough exterior are actually collateral damage of a person who is fiercely private and who has spent her life as an outed introvert.

I was raised by an incredibly brilliant woman in a loving family. I attended the premier college prep high school in my city, was an all-American athlete, and was relatively popular. I even knew Christ at the tender age of eight. I believed God with my whole heart and I still do today. Nevertheless, in the decades between then and now, I've learned that God was present in my life, not to make my life pain free, but to allow me to maneuver through the pain without giving up.

I learned about loss at a very, very young age. My mother, who is the oldest girl out of eight children, had me when she graduated high school at the age of eighteen. The first man I ever loved was not my father, but my grandfather. He was a tall and soft-spoken man who always wore fresh-pressed trousers and a shirt with impeccable shoes and a derby hat. Even when he was at home, he wore those trousers with a crisp white t-shirt. My grandmother kept my grandfather clean. I knew my Grandfather as the male role model in my house because my mom was a teenage parent. My father was her high school sweetheart—older than my mother, he was the basketball star of his high school team who went off to college. My mother was the smart and pretty brown cheerleader with the "strict" father.

After she graduated high school and her beau pursued what my mother thought was a basketball scholarship, my mother entered the workforce. My grandmother went off to clean houses every day to support me and the other six children in the home (my oldest uncle was in the military and his children were also with us) and my mother went to work at a Fortune 500 company. I was left at home with my grandfather who was too ill from cirrhosis of the liver to work. My grandmother often tells me that my grandfather, who she calls "Sonny," never smiled until I was born, his first grandchild.

I remember on one hot summer Saturday morning, my mother, grandfather, youngest uncle, and I went to an outside market. Farmers and vendors had brought their fresh produce and meat to the city to sell. This particular day was scorching and the market was crowded. Well, my mother fainted. Just two or three-years-old, I ran outside to the car to get my grandfather and uncle. My uncle picked me up as he tried to keep up with the long and purposed steps of my grandfather as I showed them where my mother had fainted. When he saw her lying there in the middle of a crowd with a white lady fanning her, my grandfather bent down and picked her up in his arms like a rag doll. In his failing health, he picked his daughter up with such ease and carried her in his arms to the car. This event may not sound like a big deal, but it is what defined a man for me. A man carries his family.

The following January, my grandfather succumbed to his battle with cirrhosis and he died. My little heart broke. I was even more devastated when the decision was made to leave me with a sitter for his funeral because my family thought I was too young to understand what was going on. I was not too young: I knew exactly what was going on. It was almost three decades later before I got closure and could tell my grandfather good-bye.

"When my mother and father forsake me, then the Lord will take me up."

—Psalm 7:10

I learned in my adult life that Sonny never really liked my father. So, my grandfather's passing opened up the door for my father to assume an active role in my life. My experience with my father was a lesson in rejection, which manifested in so many different ways. I am not sharing this recollection to bash my father, but I am sharing this in the hopes that I can help someone else break free of the rejection from his or her father.

My mother is gorgeous, brilliant, driven, and just so happens to be "darker" than what my father's mother thought was acceptable. Like me, my father was an only child. He was an only child of a woman who cherished him as if he was God and no one would ever be good enough for him. When I was five or six, I had two birthday parties. My mother threw me a party at my grandmother's house with all of my maternal family and my friends from school. There was food and laughter and fun. Neither my father nor his mother attended this party; instead they had a separate party for me at my paternal grandmother's house. Why? Because my paternal Grandmother thought my mother and her family were too "dark" to be in her house. There were no other children at the party, no family members. Just my father and paternal grandmother.

That was the only time I ever saw my father's mother and I don't even remember her name. What I do remember is how uncomfortable she made me feel. Shortly after this non-party, my father got me a beautiful dog, a husky named Jason. I guess this was his way of making peace with my mother on behalf of his mother, who I am sure could have cared less. My mother was quickly climbing the corporate ladder in her company. I'm not sure what my father did, but what I do know is that, one night, he had a horrible motorcycle accident. His accident was so bad that he came to stay with my mother and me for a while. I remember her changing his bandages and cleaning the wounds. Shortly after this accident, my father came to our house and took Jason. I didn't see my father again after that for about eight years.

The next time I saw my father was on a Saturday afternoon at the movie theaters. My mother had taken one of my best friends and me to see *Superman*. I remember standing at the concession counter, talking with my friend about what kind of candy we wanted, and I looked up to see my father staring at me from the across the lobby. He and my mother had a brief conversation, and she came over and told me to go speak to my Father.

As I stood there, he said, "Do you know who I am?"

In my twelve-year-old indignation, I answered, "Just because you left and took my dog doesn't mean I forgot who you are."

The look on my father's date's face was one I will never forget. Both she and I knew that what happened between my parents had nothing to do with her, but she knew I was not interested in meeting her. My mother was beautiful, and still is, beautiful, successful, and strong. She treated my father with respect he didn't deserve. I was forty-seven when I decided to forgive my father and I wrote him this letter:

Dear Father,
This letter I am writing to you is not out of anger or frustration, but out of pity. I feel sorry for you because you missed out on the opportunity to be a part of something amazing...me!

You missed my first track meet and the opportunity to see me break records and win medals. You missed the chance to comfort me when a boy broke my heart, to wipe my tears.

I am not even mad that you missed my high school graduation. I think it is sad that the first and maybe the only seed you have ever sown, you did not water, nurture, or prune. Who makes a deposit and doesn't watch his investment grow?

It is a sad man who has the opportunity to walk his daughter down the aisle and doesn't; who isn't present to hear the laughter of not one, not two, but three beautiful and brilliant grandchildren.

But, Wardell Jones, this letter is not about my anger or daddy issues. This letter is to tell you that I forgive you for missing out on greatness.

Once I wrote this letter, such a huge release came over me. And at that very moment I realized two very important things:

1. **My father has something to do with how I had perceived men in my life.** My father's actions didn't afford me a healthy and trusting relationship with men. Fathers teach little girls what to expect from a man. No father = no expectations. No, I do not believe "all men are dogs," but I do believe that every man owes it to his children to be there.
2. **My father was broken and couldn't give me what he didn't have.** I never saw my father again. What

has been a long and sometimes painful realization for me is that it is difficult to find something in someone that you don't already have. I believed that, in order to have a successful relationship, you had to find someone that "completes" you, rather, someone who exhibits what you desire to see in yourself. I spent much of my young adult life with the silent agony of trying to figure out what I wanted in a husband, when what I should have been looking for was his heart. The heart of a man is the most valuable and revealing thing. This was a bitter revelation for me, because it forced me to realize that I had to inspect my own heart. It was not until I was twelve years into my marriage that I realized that I was cheating my husband out of what he deserved. There was a part of me that remained buried and closed off to him because I thought that, if he knew I was hurt and broken, he wouldn't value me as his mate. I could not have been more wrong. By opening up and trusting him, I allowed him to truly love, cover, and protect me. I had to re-evaluate my marriage and do a considerable amount of forgiving. I also had to learn to let things go.

I am not finished yet. With all the victories I have secured, there are hundreds more I have yet to obtain. As I reflect on the obstacles I have overcome to date, they were not the most challenging part of my evolution. The most challenging part of my evolution is striving to be a better person than I was on yesterday.

Reflections

1. Get rid of the pain and keep the lesson: When things go wrong in our lives, we are quick to become emotional. It's okay to feel, but we can't remain emotional. Emotions are the enemy of growth. In order to process and learn the lesson, ask yourself these questions and answer them honestly:
   - Why does it hurt so bad?
   - Why am I so angry?
   - Is this anger benefitting me?
2. Do not own issues that are not your own: People act and react out of their own issues. Stop taking the offenses personally.
3. Your perception and memories are your reality: Do not allow people to guilt you out of your authentic feelings.
4. Forgiveness is not predicated on an apology: Forgiveness is about you, *not* the person you are forgiving. You must have clean and free hands to receive God's blessings.

Pray Without Ceasing

PETHRAL DANIELS

"Rejoice always, pray without ceasing, in everything give thanks; for this is the will of God in Christ Jesus for you."

−1 Thessalonians 5:16-18

"When you don't know what to do, pray; when you know what to do, pray"

−Mom

As a woman who has been blessed to become a half-century old, I have seen and experienced a lot in my lifetime. Most has been good, but like everyone, there have been circumstances, challenges, and sets backs that have shaped my thinking and life. There is one particular event that has impacted me in every area of my life, but through it all, prayer has been the sustaining factor. I always sought God, even when I was not sure if there truly was a God. I continue to seek His face, understanding that He is my power source.

My paternal grandmother had a profound impact on me. She was an extremely wise, praying woman. She had a way of making every last one of her grandchildren and great-grandchildren feel special, and there were a lot of us. She and my grandfather married very young and had seven children who all had several children of their own. Although she had not finished high school, my grandmother was one of the smartest women I knew. She always had such a wise way of showing us how to look at things through the eyes of God. She found the bright side of everything and the good in everyone; even though they may have done her wrong, she could never hold a grudge. I can still remember her saying, "Baby, you can't hold onto negativity or it will hold on to you. Let God do His job and you just pray."

Whenever I was in a bad situation, I would call my grandmother to get her wise counsel. Each time she would hear my complaint, her response was always to pray about a solution and give it all to God. She would say in her slow Southern drawl, "If you are gonna try to fix it, what do you need God for?"

Sometimes it would make me very angry that she never gave me some other advice. Just once I wanted to hear her instruct me to do something more barbaric, but of course, she never did. I knew my grandmother was a woman who knew God when the most horrible circumstance that a mother could experience confronted her and her response was to forgive and to pray. How did she do it? She looked to the Lord for His strength to endure.

"Look to Lord and His strength, seek his face always."

–I Chronicles 16:11

Pop! Pop! Pop! I heard the shots ring out. I knew exactly what that popping sound was, but who had been the target? Who did it get? What did this mean for us? My mind raced: What do I do now? Do I run or do I stay? With no time to figure it out, I grabbed my little sister and we ran for our lives. I was running and praying, running and praying. Where was my little brother? Oh God, where was he? We ran as fast as we could. Hurry, hurry, hurry. We were so scared. Hurry, hurry. "Somebody help! Help us please! God, where are You now"?

"God is our refuge and strength, A very present help in trouble"
—Psalms 46:1

It was February 13th, the night before Valentine's Day. It was chilly outside, and my sister and I stood near the furnace as we typically did when the house was cold. I was confused by the dichotomy of my emotions as I saw my dad walk into the house. He walked with his typical swag. He was such a handsome man and his confident stride paralleled his good looks. I call it the "I know I'm good-looking" swag, the same swag that used to make me swoon when I saw a good-looking man who owned the same confidence. I was happy to see my dad as I always was, but afraid of what I knew would happen next. Their voices would rise. They would argue, then my dad would hit my mom and she would cry. Daddy would be sorry for hitting her and promise he'd never to do again. Things would be great for a few weeks as he'd try to prove to mom and to us that he was sorry and that it would not happen again.

The routine was all too familiar, but I had learned how to calm my dad, so I immediately jumped into action and began to talk to him, doing what I did best: Being daddy's little girl. That usually worked and most times what could have been a major blow up was diminished to a mere disagreement, at least for the time being. That was such a heavy burden for a young girl to carry.

> *"Come to me, all who are weary and heavy burdened, and I will give you rest."*
> —Matthew 11:28

I could see the anger in my dad's eyes so I ran up to him and joyously spoke to him in a sing-song voice, "Hey, daddy! I am so glad you are home. I made you something."

I had made my daddy a card with pink construction paper, several red hearts, and lots of love. I was startled by the snap in his voice as he said, "Give it to me now, because I won't be here tomorrow." My twelve-year-old mind could not comprehend how literal that haunting declaration would become.

> *Death and Life are in the power of the tongue,*
> *And those who love it will eat its fruit.*
> —Proverbs 18:21

With my unopened card in his hands, daddy walked to the back room where my mother was and I began praying to myself as grandma had instructed me to do when I was afraid: "Oh God, please don't let them fight tonight. Please God, let them be happy." My heart was beating so fast. I knew it was not going to be good; even at that young age, I always had a sense of things, what most of the older folks call a discerning spirit. At first, it was normal voices. My ears were keen to the vibrations of every sound. Whew! I was beginning to feel relieved, but that feeling of comfort did not last very long. Time stood still as I became paralyzed with fear—there it was, just as expected, the loud voices.

My heart raced faster as the voices grew louder and louder. Then I heard it. I will never forget the sound: *Pop! Pop! Pop!* of a .22 handgun. I knew what it was the minute I heard it and all I wanted to do was run, but I could not move. I wanted to save my mom. I knew he had shot her. I had heard him on several occasions vow to my mother that he would kill her. That he would kill her and us, then kill himself. What should I do? I asked myself in a panic. Should I go back to their bedroom and save her? Should I try to take the gun so he does not hurt anyone else or himself? Or do I run?

The choice was to run. I grabbed my little sister's hand and we ran and ran and ran! We ran to the neighbor's house across the street. They would not open the door for us. I could see someone peering out the window next to the front door as we banged and banged, but no one answered. We then raced in the direction of my grandmother's house. On our way, we saw my father's aunt outside. We ran into her arms, crying, pleading for her to get help. "Please help! God please help!"

All of the next steps are blurry, but I remember being in the car with my great-aunt as she drove back to our house and there was an obvious crime scene. There were the flashing lights of police cars, an ambulance, and the local news station. All the neighbors outside gathered as they do when something tragic happens. I caught the eye of the neighbor lady from across the street who would not open her door as my sister and I pleaded and banged for help. I often wonder if my dad would still be alive if she would have just opened her door and called for help.

All the adults were caught up in the flurry of activity, and my sister and I were in the car watching it all. When I look back on that horrible night, I cannot understand why no one had the common sense to make sure my sister and I were safe somewhere so that we could not see the things that we saw that night. This scene was no place for children, but the way the car was parked allowed me to have a direct view into the small house that we called home. I could see my dad lying on the floor. He was still and the paramedics were working on him. I thought I saw him take one big deep breath and then no more. They brought him out of the house on a stretcher, then the ambulance sped off with the sirens blazing.

I remember praying to God, "Please let my mommy be okay." I was so scared. What if we had lost our mom and dad? I do not think I have ever felt that same type of fear, the fear of wondering if my mom had left this earth too. What would we do? Who would take care of us? This was too much for a twelve-year-old girl to worry about, but I knew that God was my refuge.

Soul Source

"I will say of the Lord, "He is my refuge and my fortress, my God, in whom I trust."
—Psalm 91:2

The next vivid memory I have of that evening is being at my maternal grandmother's home. My little sister and I were in the bed with her when the phone rang. I pretended to be asleep, I'm not sure why; I think I understood that all of this was too much for a child to endure. My grandmother answered the phone and I heard her explain her recollection of what happened that night. She told the other party on the phone that my mom had shot my dad.

I wanted to jump out of the bed. I wanted to know if my dad was okay—was he alive or dead? Although I had seen my dad lying on the stretcher in the ambulance and I thought he took his last breath, I was not sure and I was praying he would be okay. More importantly, I wanted to know if my mom was okay. Where was she? Did he shoot her then himself? Was she with daddy in the ambulance? Was she ever coming to get us?

I was starting to sweat, but I could not move because I needed to hear more. I could not let her know that I was awake, hearing every word she spoke. She continued to talk about my dad being taken to the hospital. I then started to put it all together: My mother had shot my father, but she was not with him. But where was she? Why was she not here with us? Then my grandmother dropped the bomb. I can hear the words like they are being said right now. She spoke through tears and sniffles: My dad had died and my mom was in police custody.

Oh my God! What will my sister, brother, and I do? Who would take care of us? I tried to silently pray every prayer I had ever known. Growing up Catholic, there are several prayers that we had to memorize and I prayed them all, "Our Father who is in heaven, hallowed be Thy name...," "Hail Mary full of Grace, the Lord is with Thee...," "Angel of God my guardian dear, to whom I love is trusted here..." I wanted to shout out to God, but I was paralyzed with fear for so many reasons. Scared of what would become of my siblings and me. Scared that my dad's family would never want to see us again because my mom had killed their favorite. Scared that my paternal grandmother, the grandmother that I loved so much, would not want to have anything to do with us.

I could feel myself trembling in the bed, lying in a pool of sweat. I wanted to fall to my knees right then and there and beg God for answers and plead with Him to make this all go away; but all I could do was lay in that pool and contribute to its depth with my silent tears. I remember my paternal grandmother had told me whenever I was afraid or felt nervous to call on the name of Jesus. I whispered, "Jesus, Jesus, Jesus" over and over again. I called on that name until I feel asleep.

In peace I will lie down and sleep, for you alone, Lord, make me to dwell in safety.

—Psalm 4:8

The next morning, I was awakened by my grandma and the nuns from my parochial school. When I rolled over, I hoped that the night before was just a terrible nightmare; but seeing the grief-stricken faces on those nuns, I knew it was not a dream. They prayed with us and let my family know that they were there for us. It took a couple of weeks before we were back in school and it seemed even longer before we would finally see our mom. Although I am told she was released only a few short days after the incident, it seemed like much longer. By this time, we were staying with family friends and we were anxiously waiting to see her. She came by their house once she was released, and I was horrified by her bruised and beaten face. I could hardly recognize her, but I dared not ask what happened. I was just happy to know she was alive.

My mother was charged with murder, but she pled not guilty and was let out on bond. With the assistance of friends and family, we made it through the funeral and the next few weeks without much fanfare. Of course, there was a trial and, again, I was filled with a stifling fear that my mom would be found guilty and would spend her life in prison, away from us. I remember not being able to concentrate in school. Hearing things on the news made me more concerned. I did not want to be with my friends; I just wanted to be near my mom. I felt like I had to spend every moment with her because there was the possibility that we could lose her too.

My paternal grandmother lifted some of my fears when she made it very clear to us that she loved us and, surprisingly enough, that she loved my mother too—she had already forgiven her. She explained that she was aware of my father's abusive behavior and she should have done more to help. I was overjoyed that she still loved us and that she wanted to make sure we were still in her life. When I say "we," it included my mom too.

What a woman of God! She was the example that God has called us all to be. She lived what she preached and was such a forgiving woman. She always said that, with God, anything is possible, and she was right.

> "For if you forgive other people when they sin against you, your heavenly Father will also forgive you."
> —Mathew 6:14

I have studied the Bible and been fed by several shepherds that I know are anointed, but my grandmother's example of forgiveness, her faith in the Word of God, and her undying trust that Jesus is the living water have had profound effects on me. She was so sincere in her love and trust in God. God was her Power Source. She has since gone on to be with the Lord, but I think of her often and hold dear to all of the lessons that she taught me. I pray that I am to my grandchildren what she was to me. I pray that I leave for them the legacy of eternal life in Jesus Christ our Lord and our Savior. I know that I will share with them some of the golden nuggets that were passed down to me, but more importantly, I will always make sure they know the power of prayer and the importance of praying without ceasing.

10 Most Important Things I Have Learned From the Experiences of My Life:

1. God is our Power Source.
2. When you don't know what to do, pray. When you know what to do, pray.
3. God is real and with us always. His silence is not His departure, but it is when He is holding us the tightest.
4. No prayer is too small or insignificant. God hears and answers prayers. He does not care if you are an innocent child or a seasoned prayer warrior. He hears you.
5. Look at problems in the light of God's power and do not look at Him only in the shadow of problems.
6. God loves you and has a plan for your life. Through prayer, we can walk the path He has for us.
7. Always call on the Lord in times of distress and praise Him in all things.
8. Developing a prayer life is essential to healthy, happy living.
9. Prayer changes everything.
10. When you have a relationship with Jesus, you have everlasting joy.

God Set Me F.R.E.E.

SONYA A. MCKINZIE

"She is clothed with strength and dignity, and she laughs without fear of the future."

—Proverbs 31:25

"The strength of a woman is not measured by the impact that all her hardships in life have had on her; but the strength of a woman is measured by the extent of her refusal to allow those hardships to dictate her and who she becomes."

—C. Joybell C

Women often dream of falling in love with Prince Charming, walking on rose petals down a long aisle, falling into the arms of her husband to be, then having children and living happily ever after. Guess what? I had that same dream. I have always wanted and dreamed of the American Dream with a husband, children, house, and the white picket fence. I needed someone to love and to return the love to me. Yes, it sounds cliché. I desired the relationship that my parents did not have but that I often saw on one of those family TV shows.

As I moved from my twenties into my thirties, I grew more afraid that after spending over a decade in a dead-end relationship that resulted in mental, physical, and emotional brokenness, I would spend the remainder of my life without a husband or children. I then received the medical reports from the doctors. "You may not be able to conceive children, and fertility drugs will likely be necessary," they told me. I lived through the truism of my biological clock and the piercing ticking that echoed inside my head. I remember the feelings of loneliness, especially when I entered my empty three-bedroom home. Like most women in their late twenties, thirties, and even forties, that biological clock intensified and grew, stronger, and louder with age. The void of true love grew profounder and tougher to null.

I wondered if I was called to singleness as described in 1 Corinthians 7:32:

> *I want you to live as free of complications as possible. When you're unmarried, you're free to concentrate on simply pleasing the Master. Marriage involves you in all the nuts and bolts of domestic life and in wanting to please your spouse, leading to so many more demands on your attention. The time and energy that married people spend on caring for and nurturing each other, the unmarried can spend in becoming whole and holy instruments of God. I'm trying to be helpful and make it as easy as possible for you, not make things harder. All I want is for you to be able to develop a way of life in which you can spend plenty of time together with the Master without a lot of distractions.*

I questioned if I was alone because I was being chastised for my poor choices or simply because I was designed to be alone, and in that aloneness, I would not bear children. I often wondered if there was something wrong with me. Where was my Adam? I would think, think, and think, and when I was not thinking, I was questioning my worth. Maybe I wasn't pretty enough. Maybe I was too broken inside because of the abuse I witnessed as a child and later experienced as a young woman. I questioned what I could do to bring my Adam to me. My small circle of friends had spouses; people passing by on the street or in a store had spouses and companions—why didn't I? I felt insignificant and lonely. I accepted men who did not love me the way I loved them, and after each broken relationship, like a fool, I would long for love again. Was my strong desire for love because my father was never present in my life? Did I have this huge void because I was told I had a low chance of conception, of breathing life into a child? What could it have been?

About ten years ago, I remember chatting with a friend that we'll call Denise, a beautiful thirty-something, filled with life, excitement, and a positive outlook on life. We often talked about our failed relationships; her vibrant view of her future and having children after marrying the perfect man was not tarnished by her bad experiences. On the other hand, my view was filled with negative thoughts and sadness; I felt like everyone was designed with a soul mate, except me. Denise and I were different yet the same: Her faith in God was unfaltering contrary to her poor choices, immoralities, and distresses. I will admit, I didn't understand the concept of speaking to God; I would question, "Why talk to

Him? He will not answer." I had little to faith in any religion at all; rarely did I pray and surrender to God—and if anyone needed prayer, it was me. I needed His guidance out of my life, which was an ugly mess.

The woman I am today is far from the woman I was yesterday. As a single woman, there were many things outside of me that influenced my thought processes and made me feel that being alone was irregular. I viewed marriage and children as a means of freeing me from a cage of unhappiness. Denise, she seemed to have a close relationship with God and an unyielding belief in Him, her eventual marriage, children, and family unit. Through her faith in God, she understood the true interpretation behind the passage in Proverbs 18:22. "Find a good spouse, you find a good life and even more: the favor of God!"

I wished that I were more like her. She had a relationship with God, she knew what discernment was, and God answered her prayers. I used to wonder, "How do I get there? Why can some people hear His voice and others cannot?" But what could I do to connect with God when I could not get the concept of prayer? How could God satisfy my needs when I had turned my back on Him for so long?

Pushing the hands of the clock forward, Denise did eventually get married. And I ... well, I eventually got married too, but my marriage was no fairytale. I married for a number of wrong reasons and none of them had anything to do with love. As a matter of fact, my marriage ended within six months after dragging me through the trenches. I stayed in the valleys for a long time before I encountered a positive peak. I have no qualms in admitting that my marriage was a failure—I jumped over that broom and, when I did, it caught fire and headed straight to Hell.

When I filed for a divorce, I was sure that that was what I needed to do. The divorce was worse than our wedding day: The man was a replay and reflection of the bad choices that I had made over and over again. Thinking back over the amount of time we dated in contrast to the lifetime of our marriage, the divorce took longer to get through than our marriage did. I experienced more heartbreak, disappointment, and loss of money in the process. I felt like a pathetic fool. Why had I allowed another person to hurt and break me? I had no answer—but God did. He knew why things happened the way that they did.

I did not realize that all I needed to do was talk to God, confess my sins, and ask for forgiveness. Proverbs 28:13 says, "You can't whitewash your sins and get by with it; you find mercy by admitting and leaving them." I needed to surrender my heart, spirit, and soul to God, and yet, I was reluctant over and over again. Something inside of me would not allow me to surrender and ask God to guide me. Had I called on His name, I would not have endured the pain that I experienced. But wouldn't you know: While shuffling my way through the divorce, I ran full speed ahead into another shipwreck.

That foolish heart of mine walked me right to the front door of another tragedy. The ink was not even dry on the divorce filing before I had let someone new come into my life and my bed. I was reading two books at one time and neither one of them made sense: Desperation and vulnerability took up residence in my heart, spirit, and soul, and I had no control over my feelings. This new man made me think God designed us for one another, and I was fooled. After all, my view of what I wanted and needed was vague and tarnished by my desire to marry and find happiness—the happiness that I molded into a pretty little gift called "love."

Replay: I was in another relationship that involved verbal abuse, lies, and disloyalty, and again, I was accepting less than I deserved. Fooled by his representative and my defenselessness, I convinced myself that he was "The One." Of course, he was not. He was just a place that I could go to in order to hide my shame and feel the emptiness that took up residence inside of me.

Thinking back, we were only in our relationship for a year when I learned that I had conceived—I was in shock and disbelief. How could I be pregnant? How on earth could it be that I was carrying a child? Seriously, I could not believe what I was seeing. I was on birth control to regulate my menstrual cycle and had polycystic ovary syndrome. The results from medical doctors and specialists alleged that I was infertile and, even with fertility drugs, the likelihood was slim. In fear, I wondered, "How could *I* have conceived a child, and more specifically, why did this happen with a man who did not appreciate, respect, or love me?"

After taking six at-home pregnancy tests (all different brands), I finally went to see my primary care physician to get professional confirmation. Those damn tests were wrong; maybe I didn't pee on the strip correctly or maybe I read the results wrong—maybe two lines meant that I was not pregnant after all?

I remember my doctor coming into the examination room of the doctor's office and saying, "Yeah, honey, you are as pregnant as you can be. The indicator on this test has two bright pink lines. Congratulations. Aren't you happy?"

I did not respond. I sat there in that skimpy gown and my knee-highs, in complete shock. I was thirty-four-years-old and in a rocky relationship with a man who did not want any more children. He had told me before that he wasn't sure that he wanted his first when he found out he was going to be a father nearly a decade prior. We had discussed children in the early months of our relationship and even marriage, but we both were fresh out of our last unions and had fallen into our situation by chance, likely a result of both of our vulnerabilities.

My doctor and I calculated and estimated that I was approximately eight weeks pregnant and, fucking scared, I wondered, "How will my baby's daddy receive the news especially after he said he did not want another child?" His finances were unstable, his mental state was unbalanced, and our relationship was a complete mess. To be honest, I could not understand why I remained in the relationship other than the sex; but then again, we weren't compatible in that area either.

I replayed my doctor's confirmation of my pregnancy. I stuttered hysterically through what seemed like a million questions. I reflected on her logical and relaxed answers while trying to calm me down—that moment was bittersweet. A large part of me wanted a baby—I always did— but I did not want one with this man. This was not in my plans—notice how I said "my," which seems pretty selfish to be concerned with only my feelings. What about my unborn child, the father, and my God? The same God who I periodically called on when things got bad? The same God who I ran from instead of running to—was this His way of blessing me or cursing me? I was so confused and alone. My mother was five and half hours away and I wanted her. I wanted to tell her and see her reaction. I wanted to cry and have her comfort me.

As I rushed out of the doctor's office, I began to recite Psalm 23: "The LORD IS MY SHEPHERD; I SHALL NOT WANT..." IT WAS QUITE THOUGHT-PROVOKING HOW, IN THAT MOMENT OF FEAR, I REACHED OUT TO GOD. THEN I quickly dialed my mother's number and said, "Mama, I am pregnant." She was silent.

I said, "Mama, did you hear me? I am pregnant."

The silence made me very uneasy and, after few more minutes, her response was, "Yea, right." This was a typical response from my mom when she felt I was joking; but when she heard the seriousness in my voice and I questioned if she was happy, she responded, "Yes, are you?" I gave her the string of reasons how this was impossible, given my condition, but God proved them wrong. I questioned her about what I should do and how I could do parenthood on such a modest salary. On top of that, I told her how hesitant I was to tell my baby's daddy of the results because he didn't want more children.

But the next call had to be to him, and I prayed that the news would not result in an argument that would leave us both angry and annoyed. When he answered the phone, he immediately asked, "How did the appointment go?" I responded, "I am pregnant. I am about eight weeks and..." I could not seem to get it out. It was vivid and clear what his reaction was.

After a silence, he asked, "What are you going to do." *That* repulsed me. It was predictable. I did a U-turn and headed to my house in Winder instead of his apartment. I could not believe that he would ask me such a question—he knew about my fertility issues with conceiving and, while I didn't pray on a daily basis, attend church every Sunday, and thump the Bible, he knew that abortion was not an option for me. I would never give up a baby—our baby!

I was infuriated. He confirmed what I already knew: He didn't want our child. I told him in a stern tone, "I am going to keep this child." His response was contrite as he said, "I'm sorry." Those two words made me hit a hard left turn. I began to drive back to his apartment. He didn't even have to ask if I was coming to his apartment, because he knew I did not want to be alone. I was afraid, scared as hell. I didn't know why at this point in my life God was blessing my womb with a child, one who was conceived in sin and outside of wedlock. But how dare I question the root of this wonderful blessing? There were so many women in the world wishing for children—hell, I was once one of them.

Later that week, I called Denise and shared my news with her. I told her about the pregnancy, and she responded, "Oh, my goodness! I am so happy for you." When we reached the question of her pregnancy status, she said, "Not yet but we are trying."

"God will bless you when it is time," I said. She had her happily-ever-after in her husband and she knew the baby was inevitable too. That was Denise: Regardless of her fertility concerns, her faith trumped negativity.

As the months passed and my miracle grew inside of me, the tension and arguments became more frequent with my baby's daddy. I needed to be in my mother's presence. The distance between Brunswick and Atlanta became very apparent because my "I need my mama" moments grew more and more recurrent as my due date grew closer. It was in those times that she encouraged me to focus on my relationship with God; I needed Him the most in this season and she pushed me towards Him.

More frequently, I read the 23rd Psalm, one of my Soul Sources. It was most familiar to my heart, spirit, and soul, and the passage was handwritten and thumbtacked to the corkboard in my office. The scripture Jeremiah 1:5—"Before I shaped you in the womb, I knew all about you. Before you saw the light of day, I had holy plans for you: a prophet to the nations—that's what I had in mind for you"—was taped to the mirror in my bathroom in the master bedroom. I would look at it each morning when I washed my face before work and before I lay down at night. This very passage helped to guide me, draw me closer to God, and encouraged me to embrace my unborn child and love her. My baby girl, I love her deeply and passionately as I love God. When I lacked faith, God breathed life into me. He didn't allow the enemy to take me through suicide, domestic violence, depression, or feelings of worthlessness. God brought me through all of those situations when I neglected to surrender myself to Him.

On March 16, 2011 at three a.m., I was in full swing of labor, preparing to meet my miracle. My mother was there when I delivered, holding my hands as we pushed to bring McKinzie into the world. She guided me towards God and, when I could not cover myself, she covered me in prayer.

As many times as I have fallen, God has picked me up in all of my imperfections. He forgave me. He loved me even when I did not love myself and he keeps on blessing me. My daughter was placed in my womb, close to my heart, and imprinted in my spirit and soul. She helped mold me into the person God destined me to be. When I think about how I went from faithless to faithful, all I can say is "Only God."

If you are reading this, you know that nothing happens by chance—all that you endure is a part of God's masterplan. In order to experience glory, we must go through struggles. We are strengthened through chaos, and without hard times, we would not have a need for God's hand.

Your dreams and ambitions are inside of you; all you have to do is look to God. He will guide you towards living as a F.R.E.E (Fearless, Renewed, Empowered, Encouraged) Spirit and Soul Survivor. Receive it, believe it, and God will bring you to it!

Birthing My Source to Live Through the Power of God

M. NICHOLE PETERS

"But the Lord is with me like a mighty warrior."
—Jeremiah 20:11

"Your breakthrough comes by training your mindset to believe in the impossible"
—Nichole Peters

The Dusk of Darkness and Reality Nightmares

I tossed and turned in my sleep as my body shook and trembled. My lungs struggled to find air as the Darkness swallowed me. It was a smothering blanket of soul-sucking blackness that laughed as I struggled. It blinded and choked me. The evil was trying to consume me, and I cried out.

Up until a decade ago, I had extreme nightmares in which I was a tiny, inconsequential human, standing outside in the cold while the world froze around me. Somehow, I knew the temperature was negative five degrees. The cold was torture. I wore no shoes, coat, gloves, or hat. My body screamed in pain as my heart struggled to pump blood. When I was younger, I sometimes longed for death. Dying seemed like a preferable option if death would bring peace.

I finally woke up as the Darkness retreated. My arms swung and flailed around as if I was fighting for my life. And maybe I was fighting against a faceless enemy to avoid becoming a casualty of an unknown war. I hated being so scared. I wanted to jump out the bed, race to the darkest corner, and hide in an old closet. Choosing to hide from Darkness by crawling into a dark space doesn't really make sense, but fear makes you forget common sense. You forget to be afraid of the creepy mice that squeak and run around your feet. You forget that there are dirty bugs and spiders hiding in the spaces around you. Sweat drips down your face and back because the adrenaline has you wired, and you're panicking and it's ridiculously hot. After all, there's no air conditioning in the housing projects. But you can't open the door. You struggle to hold on. You ignore the rodents and pests because you'd rather suffocate to death or let the mice eat you alive than to keep being tortured, night after night, by the nightmares.

I was so drained. My body muscles ached badly from fighting in my sleep, from trying to move when I felt something heavy holding me down.

Seeking the Dawn of Light (Soul)

"That light shining inside you is something powerful that shouldn't be wasted," my grandmother told me when I was ten years young and hurting. She didn't know about the nightmares or the Darkness I'd been fighting for half a decade—I didn't dare to bother my grandmother to make her upset because she had been diagnosed with congestive heart failure. She just knew something was extremely wrong and she was always there to help build me up.

Darkness had been chasing after my light for years, pushing and pulling, tempting and weakening my resolve to use my inner power for other reasons. I can remember my first few battles of will against its evil. The dark force wanted to recruit me; therefore, it refused to give me a moment of peace and banked big on my fears, anxieties, and failures to cause me major distress. Darkness called me "ugly," and I started to hate my smooth, dark skin. Darkness called me "stupid," and I believed it.

In the projects where I grew up, I had some elders who looked down on me. I would bring my radio outside and dance my problems away. Some would say, "Boy, the way she shakes her behind, she will be pregnant before she graduates from school—if she manages to graduate at all." Some of my associates I went to school with who lived in brick homes would look down on me and laugh because I lived in the projects; I was nobody to them. I started believing the dark, evil thoughts mixed with all the people who rejected me and let me down, whispering that I was worth nothing.

I had never been an all-A's student, but despite being haunted by Darkness, I was full of creative energy and powerful visions. I loved to dance and sing at the top of my lungs. I enjoyed school and loved writing stories until my elementary grade teacher flat out told me I wasn't good enough to be an author because I had deficits in reading comprehension. I had to take Title I classes for reading and English. My young spirit didn't sit well with this teacher at all. "Why not show me ways I could do it even with my challenges?" I thought. "Why stick in this class for one full hour where we hardly do anything but color in coloring books?"

I thought a teacher should be one of the main leaders of your life, someone who should tell their students, "You can do it!" But instead of encouraging me, she was patronizing and mean. She didn't even realize my heart was breaking. I felt doomed on my dreams and disliked her with every fiber of my soul. One time, she made me so mad that I screamed out loud, "You're the Devil! You're an asshole!" I got a butt-spanking, plus I was on punishment for weeks.

I will never forget that long walk from Northside Elementary. When I crossed the small bridge on the way home, I stopped and cried harder than I had after any of my horrifying nightmares. I stared down at the water below me and thought about jumping right in. I could float away. Nothing was going right in my life. My mother was always working, and when she got off, she came home and cooked, helped her children with homework, made sure we were in bed at a decent hour, and saw about her sickly mother every single day. The only days she had off was Sundays. She still cooked delicious, big meals every Sunday for her family and some of the kids who needed to eat in the projects. I could feel Ma'dear's pain when she was extremely tired and weak, and I used to ask God to give her strength. I just didn't want to put any more on her. My beautiful Queen was already bearing enough, and my father was never around when I needed him the most.

On top of it all, I couldn't sleep without having nightmares, and now my teacher had expressed, in so many words, that I would be a complete failure or a dummy. I wept fat, rolling tears on that bridge for nearly a half hour, just looking down with a racing, suicidal mind, wishing for peace.

I was about an hour late getting home from school. My grandmother was waiting with her little switches (very small tree branches that every child who lived in the hood in the eighties mostly caught a whooping with), because she didn't play. Not coming home from school on time was a major rule broken. She started swinging and quickly noticed that hitting me on my behind the first few times hadn't gotten me jumping and screaming. So, she turned me around, took one good look into my eyes, and knew I was troubled. I had been numb to every lick and couldn't bear any more punishment. I finally broke down and told my grandmother the whole truth. Granny grabbed me by my chin and pulled my face up.

She said, "Nikki, look me in my eyes. So what, baby, if you are different than others? You are created from a totally different cloth, uniquely made the way you are for a reason. I knew this day was coming soon. Accept the gifts Father God has given you. You know the mighty warrior visions you used to tell Granny about? Others may have more book sense than you, but do they have common sense? Wisdom is the best gift. You don't even know how much wisdom you've got at this young age. Until you know God's plan, see the good in yourself instead of the weaknesses. I might not be here to witness all your good days and works because I am getting older, but I will always be at your side. So promise me something, Nichole. Never let no human belittle or tell you what you cannot do. The enemy wants to take you out because he knows you are a force to be reckoned with. You must fight hard to persevere. You will do it."

At that very moment, I felt so alive. My will to survive was like iron shaping my spine. It was a Hallelujah praise moment. My heart pumped hard and I shouted, "I can become a warrior!" I started praying and that gave me hope.

God's voice was my confirmation that I would survive. Often when I got finished praying, I would hear the Almighty's voice tell me, "Go forth with my message, princess." John 4:4 (KJV) says, "Ye are of God, little children, and have overcome them: because greater is He that is in you, than he that is in the world." I will never forget how hard my heart pumped. I felt like Niki-woman in my victorious warrior dreams again. I stayed prayed up, and that alone gave me hope and strength. Despite everything that was thrown my way, I did make it and graduated on time without a baby.

This doesn't mean I didn't falter. Some days after I prayed, the inner beast tried to tear at my guts and made me curl up in defeated despair. I tried my best to fight off the dark forces, to keep the unwanted shade of Darkness from smearing not only my face, but my entire body. I longed to break free from every chain. As I grew older, I knew I needed to pray more to birth my inner warrior. But what haunted me was strong, overwhelmingly more powerful than my inner light, and it whispered its intentions. Evil wanted me to serve as general on its frontline, instead of being a true warrior for God. I was tired of agony and pain, and slipped up by throwing in the towel—a huge mistake!

As the saying goes, when you are weak, you are beat. I became a bitter young adult who felt betrayed, powerless, and unloved. I had forgiven my father and we were very close again until he became ill. He died at a time when any young daughter would need her father's advice the most. I was five months pregnant with my first child. My grandma, my hero, was constantly in and out of CCU. Ten months later, I lost her too. I was barely an adult and I couldn't think straight. I ended up flunking out of college twice and just couldn't focus.

During my grief, I made so many wrong turns. Let me name a few: I fell deeply in love with an undercover drug dealer, subscribing to a street life of dirty money and sin; I was in more domestic violence disputes, getting used and abused; I became a single parent for my amazing disabled children; and I started hanging around with the wrong crowds and picked up on major bad habits from the streets. I felt cold and destitute, and rejected anybody who tried to tell me anything by having an "I don't give a got-damn" attitude.

I remember the second time I came close to suicide. In my weakness, I accepted the spiritual darkness as it clouded my mind, body, and spirit, leaving me brokenhearted and alone. I felt that, because of all the mistakes, I deserved the pain and punishment. I will never forget that horrible day I literally ran toward death, from the living room down the hallway to my Ma'dear's bedroom. I opened all her drawers, looking for her pistol, but her gun wasn't in its customary spot. After fully searching her bedroom, I decided to seek peace another way. I decided to overdose on my prescription pills and chose the bathtub as the best place to sacrifice my life.

I loved to praise and worship in the tub, and for some reason, I felt God would forgive and accept me into Heaven if I killed myself in that tub since He knew my pain more than anybody. I sat there, soaking in both water and tears before grabbing two pill bottles and a cup of orange juice. I twisted off the caps and was ready to pour out a fatal handful of pills, but something whispered, "Try to pray first." I wanted to protest because, every time I'd tried to pray, I just couldn't get it right. But the voice sounded like my granny's. Her angel's voice convinced me to shift in that tub until I was on my knees.

I pleaded my case to Father God. I prayed so hard, I literally started speaking in another tongue. My bath water cooled and changed color. It looked like milk and honey. I was in pain but I couldn't stop praying and praising the love of God. My bath towel turned into a microphone, my mirror became my congregation, and my reinforced voice became the guide and power I needed to heal. I urged myself to respect life's blessings. I needed to live, to shine, and to give all my darkness to the Lord.

At this low point, I found my inner strength! I started praise dancing and shouting until both bottles were knocked over and pills spilled all over the floor. I knew then there was a God! That night I promised God that, no matter what I went through, I would never give up. No darkness would ever hide my glorious light ever again.

Getting Out of the Darkness

God blessed me with an extremely strong gift that has been with me since birth. It is the spiritual gift of discernment with which I can sense and distinguish spirits. I can use spiritual sight to appraise a person or a situation and see the truth. The enemy recognized my potential strength and targeted me from the time I became mature enough to judge right from wrong. Evil wanted my gifts from God.

As a teenager, I just didn't recognize that the war against Darkness had started. It whispered in my dreams and turned happy thoughts to nightmares. It tortured me mentally and attempted to break me. Evil wanted to rule me and I existed in an exhausted state of depression and fear. I thought that the only way to find peace was to fight and give into bad judgment. The hell with that—now that I know better! I reference back to my Bible, especially Isaiah 60:1-5, and I understand that you can fight back the darkness. I read Psalms 91 daily and let it feed my soul as a daily source of get-out-of-the-darkness vitamins.

As I grew older, the Darkness attacked my ability to live well, mentality, physically, emotionally, financially, and most of all, spiritually. But not this time! I was old enough to know it was time to get out of the Darkness and help others. It was time for me to get on the frontline for my rightful mission granted by God.

I witnessed the worst storm in America's history. Hurricane Katrina crashed through my hometown, leaving us with very little supplies. I was nearly eight months pregnant with my fourth child. FEMA gave us the option to relocate to another state. I was ready for a change in my life and was excited to take the opportunity to move away from the bad elements I was trying to avoid. I wanted a second chance and full responsibility for my life.

I started going back to church. I sang praises to the heavens and studied the Bible, and yes, I had to depend on public assistance, but I knew it was for only a limited time. I wanted to break the generational curse in my family by letting go of government assistance that I'd depended on for most of my life. I wanted my kids, who had challenges, to be able to go to great schools so they could defeat their cognitive impairments and grow up to be somebody one day.

I will never forget riding in that U-Haul. All I could say to myself was that a change was coming and I was getting far away from all the Darkness. I smiled with joy the whole ride to Texas. I thanked my Ma'dear and gave her so many hugs and kissy-kisses for being there for me and my children when I was out there in the wilderness. Ma'dear never gave up on me. I wanted to show my children and family who mean the world to me that, if I can do it, you can too, no matter what disabilities you may face. My fighting warrior spirit just wouldn't give up. I decided to not give into the Darkness. Instead of destroying my life's purposes, I decided to live for them.

Snatch Back Your Happiness and Believe in Your Dreams

Joy is essential to your life. Master the art of containing the inner beast. The Darkness tried to make me believe that my Highest Power God didn't love me, that I was nothing but a filthy rag. Bull crap! I decided to snatch back my happiness. God's voice says to me, "I am your Father! I am who I am and you are who I say you are. Do not fear." He equips me in every way, even though I am one of His imperfect vessels. We all remember that Moses had so many doubts and inner demons too. In Exodus 4:10 (NIV), Moses said to the Lord, "Pardon your servant, Lord. I have never been eloquent, neither in the past nor since You have spoken to Your servant. I am slow of speech and tongue." Moses listened to God's voice, not the darkness, and he accomplished miracles.

My miracle? The great I Am said I would be an awesome writer and speaker despite my disability. I have become a successful bestselling author, publisher, and international motivational speaker with over 60,000 followers who communicates to women all over the globe. Snatch your power back by experiencing happiness through letting go and letting God. Even when a person does you wrong, forgive them. When you don't forgive others, you open mental and emotional doors to bitterness and hate. Think positive by believing. I have my own Believe In Your Dreams Publishing and TV network now. One of my shows will be powered by RHG Media and VoiceAmerica.

You must believe to achieve. Once you set a goal and get a small taste of peace, positivity, purpose, passion, prosperity, perseverance, and prayers, you will never go back to dwelling in the miserable darkness within. I have witnessed manifestation like never before. But you must fight! The warrior in me finally battled back to live all my joyous childhood visions and dreams. I am living my dreams through Father God's grace and mercy, and this is what I call winning. I became the warrior Niki-Woman who is the black, soul-sista version of Wonder Woman, who wants to save anyone going through darkness, distress, and violence. The bracelet I wear every single day is truly my protection. It reads, "God Is Big Enough."

My eleven tips to heal your soul sources and welcome in letting go and letting God:
1. Welcome prayer into your life daily.
2. Believe in your dreams.
3. Rock your power of change and positivity.
4. Get connected spiritually, mentally, physically, and emotionally.
5. Stay joyous and release all fear.
6. Rebuke the enemy and he shall flee.
7. Make love your greatest passion for others.
8. Reach back and help others.
9. Stay true to who you are and release all masks.
10. Become unstoppable by speaking life.
11. Trust God to bring you out of every war!

Where Does Your Confidence Lie?

KIM RENEE SAMUELS

"But blessed is the one who trusts in the Lord, whose confidence is in Him"
—Jeremiah 17:7

*"I can be changed by what happens to me,
but I refuse to be reduced by it."*
—Maya Angelou

When I look at my surroundings and see what God has made, I can see He is much bigger than life. When I look back at where God has brought me from, I know God had His hand on me and spared my life. The fact that I am breathing and woke up this morning tells me God is real.

The purpose of your life is far greater than your own personal fulfillments, your family, your career, your peace of mind, your dreams, or even your happiness. We must realize it all starts with God and it is important that we keep this in perspective.

Perspective is powerful. Often, our trials are magnified and our blessings are minimized. The enemy would like for you to believe just that. He comes to kill, steal, and destroy

(John 10:10). He wants you to dwell on your trials and disappointments. He wants to discourage you and make you feel as though you are a failure. The enemy is a liar, deceiver, and an accuser.

How many times have you felt like you are not worthy of God? How many times have you felt you could not be God's disciple because your prayer life isn't strong enough? How many times have you felt like you couldn't be a minister because you can't recite a scripture or remember Biblical stories? How long have you been waiting for God to heal your body and take away the hurt from your heart and mind? Perhaps it's been so long that you have cast doubt or felt like giving up, but that is exactly the way the enemy wants you to see things.

We can't allow the enemy to take advantage of us when we are down and weak. You must cast your cares on the Lord and not give up. The Bible tells us to cast all your cares upon Him, because He cares for you (1 Peter 5:7).

Now, put things into perspective and look around. It isn't about you—see beyond yourself and know that your trials are temporary. It will be all over in the morning. Know that this too shall pass. Our disappointments are a drop in eternity; a cup compared to the deep well of Living Water we can access. Jesus said in John 4:14, "Whoever drinks of the water that I shall give him will never thirst. But the water that I shall give him will become in him a fountain of water springing up into everlasting life."

We must learn to look past our cup of trials and tap into God's never-ending well of blessing! The cup is good; it serves its purpose and leaves us thirsty. But as long as we keep trying to satisfy our thirst in our own might, we will be desperate for more. On the other hand, those who "hunger and thirst for righteousness," the Bible says, "shall be filled" (Matthew 5:6).

When you find God, you learn to trust in the Lord. The Bible says, "Trust in the Lord with all your heart and lean not on your own understanding; in all your ways acknowledge Him, and He shall direct your paths" (Proverbs 3:5-6). After you have put things into perspective, have confidence in the Lord. Stop doubting yourself and, instead, delight yourself in the Lord. He shall give you the desires of your heart (Psalm 37:4).

I had no choice but to trust God, but it was after many disappointments. During the time of my parent's divorce, there was a lot of strife, confusion, division, disappointments, and trials, which caused me heartache and despair. My cup of trials felt like a ton of bricks. After the divorce I was subjected to much negativity and corruption. I was molested and, fifty percent of the time, I was left to raise myself and my siblings. It felt like the hurt would never go away, as if a dagger was being stabbed into my heart over and over again. It left me in a state of trauma and I felt like my insides had been turned out. I found myself looking for answers, asking how this could be and why I simply didn't belong.

I would sometimes pray that God would remove me from my family. I tried to tell them what was going on, how men my mother knew would continue to prey after me, the vulgar and raunchy things they would say. Each day was a battle and the enemy presented himself to me in many disguises. He wore smiles and expressed kindness and love during the day but when the sun set, they became evil doers, cunning, sly, and slick. Some were drug pushers and thieves in the night. I remember sleeping with a gun under my pillow, afraid that the man who molested me would come for me again. I was fourteen-years-old and scared, fearful of the men I was around. I always wondered who would come for me next and snatch me up and hurt me.

When I had the chance to tell or the nerve to yell, no one would believe me. No matter how loudly I would scream and how the windows might shatter, those who mattered would not hear me. When no one listened, I would cut them with my tongue. I was rebellious; I fought back and tried to change people by telling those who should know better what was right and what was wrong. But it never changed anything; instead I was misunderstood even more. I became the troubled child.

Thank God there was a seed planted in me. I knew who God was. I knew I could pray and prayer would change things. I knew there was power in the name of Jesus. The Lord called us to His own glory and excellence, and I knew that God could bring me out of the corruption that I was living in. The Bible says, "His divine power has granted to us all things that pertain to life and godliness, through the knowledge of him who called us to his own glory and excellence, by which he has granted to us his precious and very great promises, so that through them you may become partakers of the divine nature, having escaped from the corruption that is in the world of sinful desire" (2 Peter 1:3-4).

All that I have been through brings me to what I struggle with today and have done so for the last twenty-five years: Lupus. How you handle life and its curve balls can affect you physically, emotionally, and psychologically. I really believe the trauma in my earlier life brought the onset of Lupus. I call it the big question mark disease. No one really knows where lupus originated from or how anyone gets the disease. I have heard some say it was due to some traumatic time in your life that left your body weak, which causes the body to create more antibodies than needed. Those antibodies eventually go after the good tissue, leaving you with an autoimmune disease also called disconnective tissue disorder.

When I heard that trauma could be the root, it made sense. Most of my childhood and adult life were full of traumatic moments. I remember sitting in my bathroom at one point, trying to erase myself with my mind, trying to go away or disappear. It was a very painful moment and I wanted to remove myself from it all and everyone that was a part of the pain. I was so full of hurt and I did not want to live a second longer, but I knew it was wrong to kill myself. So I tried to do it with my mind, thinking it wouldn't be the same as physically killing myself. I've always wondered if that moment was the actual onset of this horrible disease.

Weeks or a couple of months later, I began to feel pain in my joints. It started with my hands and, before I knew it, the pain appeared almost anywhere in my body. I had no idea what was going on. I experienced pain and swelling in my hands so bad that I would take an ice bandage and wrap my hands up because I didn't know what else to do. After the onset of a flare, I would attempt to make a doctor's appointment, but it would take a couple of days, sometimes weeks before I got in to see the doctor. By the time I got to the office, the swelling had gone down and the doctors had nothing to examine. So who looked like the crazy one? Whenever I would go to the emergency room, they would always ask, "Did you hit your hand on something?" and insist on doing x-rays. I would tell the doctors time and time again that I didn't hit my hand—something else was wrong. Needless to say, nothing would come out of the ER visit except an expensive bill.

As days went on, my symptoms got worse. I couldn't pick up a fork or pencil, not even a safety pin. I couldn't move my fingers without excruciating pain in every joint in my fingers and hand. I was paralyzed and unheard, just like when I was a child, screaming for someone to hear me when men were hurting me. Then it dawned on me: I was still screaming for someone to help me. Screaming as loud as I can and still no one heard me. All anyone could say was "I don't know what to do" or "I wish I could help." No one had answers or could help the pain go away. I continued to suffer.

I found it very hard to explain to someone who had no clue as to what I was dealing with. It is almost as if you have to feel the pain to understand it. Everyday, my struggle got harder and the pain increased. I was either in pain or feeling sick, sometimes both. In the meantime, everything looked fine on the outside, because Lupus can be invisible. Although I felt like giving up, something in me pushed me to keep moving. It had to be God. I continued to try and live a normal life, and would pray and ask God to give me strength. However, I don't recall having conversations with God asking Him to heal me. I think I was still operating in my own might. Isn't that funny how we can ask God to provide for some of our needs but don't think that He can provide all of them? His word says,

"But my God shall supply all of your needs according to his riches in glory by Christ Jesus" (Philippians 4:19).

As time went on, my family moved to Bermuda and I pursued employment. I was able to get a job but I had to go to the immigrations office in order to work. This was all taking place in early summer and it was extremely hot. One day, I took a bus to town and walked to the immigrations office, sweating bullets. It was so hot that people were walking around with cold packs, fans that blow water, and rags to constantly wipe the sweat from dripping off their bodies. Once I got into the line, I began to feel faint and, next thing I knew, I fell to the floor. The man standing behind helped me up and I went to the restroom to throw water on my face, thinking I just got a little overheated.

I managed to get through the immigration process and started my way back home when I realized I couldn't walk without feeling like I was going to fall down again. I then sat on the curb with my head down, sweating profusely, praying to God, "Please help me get home. I can't even lift my head." A lady noticed I needed help and put me in her cab and took me home. Once I got home, I realized I was still burning up. Being that it was so hot, I had no idea I had a fever. The doctors on the base had no clue. They called my husband and rushed me back into town to the only hospital on the island.

All I can remember is the ice packs and cold rags the nurses applied to my body, along with an IV. The doctors were having a hard time breaking the fever and I was slowly slipping away. I was told this one doctor who had flown in from England examined me and reviewed my case at which time he realized I had lupus. That man was sent from God.

I should have been gone but God spared my life at that very moment. I am so glad I know Jesus. I was just a baby in Christ but I knew enough to call on His name.

When I got through my near death experience, I knew God had a reason and a purpose for my life. Understanding God's purpose took a while. There were times when I would ask God, why? Was it because of what I said to hurt those who hurt me? I pleaded and pleaded with God to set me free. I confessed my sins every day to make sure I was right with God and pleaded with Him to heal me. I still had days when I couldn't use my hands or walk. Some days, I couldn't get out of bed to go to the bathroom. My children had to pull me to the toilet. It was a horrible feeling, and sometimes, it still is to know that there are so many things I'd like to do but am prevented from doing by this disease.

This made me think, maybe it isn't about what I want to do and it is all about what God has for me to do. I had to change my way of thinking. I first had to accept that, any and all hurt I may have caused, God has forgiven me for, once I confessed my sins and surrendered to Him. When I did that, I earned the right to have joy. The gift of joy is your right as a believer and follower of Jesus Christ. In fact, it says in Nehemiah 8:10, "The joy of the Lord is my strength."

Of course, the enemy wants you to feel unworthy, beat down, and condemned for things you have done in the past. He wants to rob you of your joy. Remember, he comes to kill, steal, and destroy. But we have all made mistakes. We have fallen short one way or another. We all rebelled against God's authority over our lives. But we are also blessed because our sins have been forgiven. Once I realized joy was mine and a right and privilege from God, no one and nothing could take away my joy.

Today, I get out of bed with joy in my heart. Even though it hurts to get up some days, I give God praise—thank You, Lord! I look back on where He has brought me from and I praise Him more and more, because in spite of my pain, I am still here and I still have joy. I am going to praise Him because I still have breath to do so, and I am a living testimony.

At the very beginning, I said God is much bigger than you and me, and the purpose of your life is far greater than your own personal fulfillments. Knowing that, you can allow God to use you and have His way. God uses me through my affliction, and to receive His blessings, I have to repent daily. We serve a forgiving God, and we need to ask for His forgiveness daily. It is important that your heart and attitude are right. We must also align ourselves with the word of God, because little by little, the enemy seeks to draw us away from God's presence. The Bible says, locust eats the leaves, the caterpillar eats the fruit of the tree, the cankerworm eats the bark, and the palmerworm eats the roots (Joel 2:25). We must repent so the Lord can restore the years that have been eaten away, years the enemy has taken.

True repentance is the key to divine restoration. We must go back to where it started, to the passion of when we first believed. We must acknowledge His anointing on our lives to cast out evil ways, give the devil no place in our mind, body, and soul, and to live a holy and separate lifestyle. The cares of this life will cause us to lose the fire, but we need the fire of the Holy Spirit in our hearts! The word says that this battle is not mine, but it belongs to the Lord (2 Chronicles 2:15). That Holy fire keeps me fighting. Knowing that God has my back ensures me that my own testimony has been a blessing for me. The fact that there was a time when I couldn't feed myself and now I can gives me the hope and joy that I have been speaking of.

With that said, I believe God is using me through my affliction to not only bless myself but others as well. Many times when I am standing before the congregation and even when I am in the fields working, I'm dealing with pain and discomfort. Lupus has also brought on continence issues and I can feel seepage of my bowels releasing, not always enough to soil my garments, but enough to make me uncomfortable. There are some days I just don't want to deal with it. I have cried about it saying, "God, there's so much in life I want to accomplish. There's so much I feel I will never be able to do. I want to live free from all of this and not have to think about my day, constantly worrying if I will be healthy and have the energy and strength to make it through. I want to be able to make plans and follow through."

Well, the truth is that I can make it through, because I have given it to God. I am not going to worry; I am going to pray instead. If it is big enough to worry about, it's big enough to pray about. Jesus wept, but He sacrificed His life. God is much bigger than me and the purpose of my life is far greater than my own personal fulfillments. He uses me for His way.

My confidence lies with God.

God Will Give You Beauty for Ashes

DORETTA GADSDEN, RN

"To appoint to them that mourn in Zion, to give to them beauty for ashes, the oil of joy for mourning, the garment of praise for the spirit of heaviness; that they might be called trees of righteousness, the planting of the LORD, that he might be glorified."

— Isaiah 61:3

My life today is so different from the place of incest, drug addiction, and hopelessness that I came from. Today I'm a registered nurse, a wife, a mother, and a grandmother who loves her family and who is loved. I have lived a relatively healthy life for the past twenty-four years with an AIDS diagnosis. God has been good to me. He has walked me through some dark and scary places. One of the shadows that I often have had to dance with is the spirit of depression. I know I'm not the only one who has felt like a dark cloud follows her around or has experienced the feelings of hurting so bad inside that she must cut herself to *relieve* the pain. I'm not the only one who has felt like even the smallest task takes painstaking effort.

One gift that I value and love about myself is the ease with which I can share my truth. It used to make my husband hold his breath, waiting for what inner feeling I would share with someone. I believe we walk through valleys in life to grow and be molded into someone better, and when that happens, it becomes an elixir for someone's soul.

The feelings of depression started when I was young. My father molested me from the age of six to ten. I told my aunt, great grandmother, and mother. My paternal grandmother raised me because my mother was only fourteen when I was born and I was her second child. However, she was not present when I disclosed what my father was doing to me. My father kept me from talking to my great grandmother with whom I was close. I was getting older and became more rebellious toward him touching me in places that were not his to touch. They all sat there with stunned faces after I told them what had been happening in my father's and stepmother's homes.

Soon, my mother took me to live with her for a short period while my father was charged with child abuse. In the middle of the court case, I believe she became overwhelmed with the whole situation and returned me back to my father's family, and they immediately made me drop the charges and say I made the story up. I felt so alone in the world and started hanging out with much older people, using drugs like marijuana and having sex at twelve-years-old. I became pregnant by a man, twenty-four years old, and with whom I ran away with to California. My family created a plan to get me back to New York by telling me that my great grandmother was sick. I returned to discover she wasn't ill at all; it was just a way to get me back home.

I never felt safe or seen by my family. I moved through my young life feeling invisible and not valued. Feeling so sad inside, I wanted to scream for a long time. I felt that, if I could scream hard enough and long enough, I would stop hurting. The sadness felt embedded in me.

My grandmother allowed my father to talk her into making me have an abortion when I was six months pregnant. The thought that this man had any say in my life made me feel like nothing. *Roe v. Wade* was just passed by the Supreme Court and, when I look back, I feel I was one of the first to go through with killing a child that had been rumbling in my stomach. I was so young and felt so alone. No one stayed with me through this horrible ordeal.

The person who showed the most kindness during the abortion was the African American doctor who talked kindly to me and made me promise that I would never come this way again. I promised him. The needle he put in my stomach was huge and painful, full of solution that induced labor and killed my child. I didn't understand anything that was going on. After it was over, my grandmother came to pick me up. I was numb. I don't recall her asking me how I felt or displaying any concern about what I had just gone through. My grandmother wasn't a mean woman, but she never showed me much affection. When I think back about my grandmother and the court case, I know she had conflicted feelings and did not know how to turn her son in. She told me this just before she died and asked me to forgive her. I already had.

Shortly after, I was sent to a reform school by the name of Holy Cross in Rhinebeck, New York. There, I met many people from all walks of life: White, Filipino, and Jewish to name a few. There were kids from everywhere. I got to see how other nationalities lived. And that was where my life began to shift. I was presented with a world of possibilities that I had never seen before.

One of the many things I loved about being in upstate New York was the quiet. Even though there were many others around, I always felt alone and that is when I started talking to God. No formal prayer at first, just feeling His presence. When I prayed, talked, and cried to Him, I would feel lifted. Cared for. Protected. Not totally alone.

God sent a woman by the name of Maggie to be my counselor. She talked to me and took me off campus often. She could see that I felt damaged and ashamed at how my family had treated me, like I had done something wrong and not my father. In the end, he was not put away but I was. Maggie taught me to be kind to myself and to not judge myself by what had happened. To see myself as whole, important, and worthy of love. Maggie was a gift from God because all the encouragement and love she gave me has always stayed in my heart.

Eventually, Maggie left. Holy Cross changed and the quality of counselors shifted. The horses were gone, tennis court closed, and they started sending more inner city kids. It was no longer diverse and the quality of care was different. I was soon sixteen and pregnant again. My oldest daughter was born, but due to my inexperience, she was raised with her paternal grandmother and father. At nineteen, I started shooting heroin to dull the sadness and depression that consumed me with pain. It was the only time I felt normal and whole. Heroin made me into a confident and bold woman, not shy and timid as I had always been. But then, it turned on me like drugs are known to do. I just wanted a way for the pain to get out of my body; it just needed an opening. I had thoughts of cutting myself. Thoughts are powerful forces if we entertain them.

This is when I really started my relationship with God. The depression and drug abuse was too big for me. I felt trapped and started reading a little green Bible someone had given me. I carried it everywhere. I would tie up my arm, shoot up, and then pull out my Bible, pleading for God to save me. I was in hell and I did not know how to get out. But I knew I was meant for more than the life I was living. I would read the sixth Psalm over and over again:

O Lord, do not rebuke or punish me in Your anger, nor discipline me in Your wrath. Have mercy on me and be gracious to me, O Lord, for I am weak (faint, frail); heal me, O Lord, for my bones are dismayed and anguished. My soul [as well as my body] is greatly dismayed. But as for You, O Lord—how long [until You act on my behalf]? Return, O Lord, rescue my soul; save me because of Your [unfailing] steadfast love and mercy. For in death there is no mention of You; in Sheol (the nether world, the place of the dead) who will praise You and give You thanks? I am weary with my groaning; every night I soak my bed with tears, I drench my couch with my weeping. My eye grows dim with grief; it grows old because of all my enemies. Depart from me, all you who do evil, for the Lord has heard the voice of my weeping. The Lord has heard my supplication [my plea for grace]; the Lord receives my prayer. Let all my enemies be ashamed and greatly horrified; let them turn back, let them suddenly be ashamed [of what they have done].

I ached. I felt frail. My enemies were my thoughts and feelings of sadness and unworthiness. But I know God was listening. This Psalm felt like it was written for me.

Shooting drugs was torment but I did not know a way out. So I just kept praying every time I used. Praying and believing it would be my last time. The people in the shooting gallery would get upset and say I was mocking God. But I was crying out for strength. Today, I'm still here and most of them are decreased.

One day while sitting in the shooting gallery after I had used my drugs and prayed, God said to me, "You are just passing through. I will bring you out of here." In that moment, I did not know how: I was dirty and disheveled, going from one family member's home to another. But I believed that God would answer me.

A short while later, I met an angel of a man who saw me. The me who was under the depression and drug addiction. The me who was whole, loving, and kind and just did not know how to find my way. He loved me until I learned to love myself. He was my mirror, my friend, my present from God to see me through to the other side of life. He put me through nursing school after I went through rehabilitation from drugs and, though we are not together today, I know God put him in my life to guide me out of the hell that was my life at that time.

Though I got off of drugs and started a new life, what I know for sure is that healing comes in layers. The outside was easy to clean up with my angel friend's love and support. My insides still hurt. I was holding onto bitterness and anger for many years toward the women in my family who should have protected me from my father. And that is fuel for depression. You cannot be happy and live a full life if you harbor ill feelings towards others. It is like an open wound that you keep pouring alcohol into, only you are the one who is burning and they are moving on with their lives.

For many years, even after my life appeared whole, I would have to catch my thoughts. Feelings of sadness would hit me if I entertained them for too long. I would sometimes compare myself to others, feeling like they were better than me, smarter, moved faster in their business, or raised their children better. That last one would really get me. I would start to question what the point of living was. During those times, everything felt like an effort.

Meanwhile, when I look back, I see that I am a woman who God brought out of drug addiction, has lived a healthy life with an AIDS diagnosis, and has a family who loves her. It is during times like these that I have to look at my thoughts. Am I listening to my mind and not relying on the God who adores me, the God who has protected me and my loved ones? I must look at whom and what am I listening to. I must question: Am I forgetting my reference points?

I have been in hell and God has brought me through. I have been sick and I'm now healthy in the face of an illness that has killed many of my friends. My youngest daughter is still in my life despite her entering foster care and then being adopted because I did not get myself together fast enough. God placed her in a home right in the next building to my mother. She has blessed me with six grandchildren.

Depression can visit anyone despite your blessings. I fell into a depression about six months ago. I had just published a best-selling book on Amazon and was invited to speak at several events with other women. Things seemed to be going well. Then, out of nowhere, I decided I needed to back up. A heaviness came over me again. I felt like I was off-track, even though things seemed to be going well. I prayed and was lead to be still. In my mind, I believed my book would become irrelevant if I waited. But God was telling me something different, so I listened.

I kept working at my job, serving my patients the best way I knew how. That part of my job I like. I'm a healer—that I know. I know I make a difference in my patient's lives. When I'm with them and teaching them something that could save their lives, I feel on purpose. Today, I'm doing well. Feelings of depression may visit again; it's something that I have lived with for most of my life. My advice to those suffering the same is to dance with it. I have found my way of living my best life with it for now.

If you have experienced the heaviness of depression, these are some of the tools in my treasure chest you may want to try:

- Create time for meditation and prayer: Allow yourself the space and time to feel, pray, and listen to God.
- Journaling: This activity will allow you to freely get in touch with what you are feeling.
- Be mindful of sugar intake: Sugar can bring your mood up and make you crash, while giving you feelings of heaviness.
- Support system: Have someone you can talk to when you are feeling heavy. Someone who will not judge you.

- Medication/Herbs: Research what best works for your depression. If medication is the way, take them. If you are choosing herbs, please be mindful of the interactions with your other medications and foods.
- Exercise: Even if it is taking a brisk walk each day, exercise gets the feel-good hormones working for you and will lift your mood.
- Practice forgiveness: Holding onto old hurts and resentment keeps you stuck and mired in the past. It is over and now you must give yourself the love and kindness you wanted from others. Love yourself by forgiving.
- Write letters to the people who you feel have harmed you: You don't have to deliver it. Just get your feelings out.
- Create ways to have fun: Find what makes your heart sing and do it often.
- Thoughts: Be mindful of what you are keeping your mind on. When you ruminate on things you think you lack or are out of your control, you add to feelings of hopelessness.
- Gratitude: List the many things that are good in your life. Each morning before you get out of bed, just start thanking God that you have another day: Your body is functioning the best it can, you have food to eat, and all other things that one may take for granted.
- Affirmations: Create affirmations that lift you and speak to the life you want to live.
- They are just feelings and it will pass: Just keep yourself moving, even in small ways.

- Professional help: If you begin to feel like you will harm yourself, reach out to a professional who can help you and talk to you.

There is nothing too big for God. He has instilled the power within us to overcome anything. All we need do is spend time in His presence. Keep in mind of what you want to feel and act like, because you are well on your way to getting there. No way am I saying it is easy, but with the tools above and through standing in prayer, depression can be handled.

What I know is that, today, I'm not a drug addict or a lost and emotionally broken woman. I no longer live in shame of the incest or any part of my past. God has taken all my feelings of brokenness and allowed me to see myself through His eyes. He took my prayers and turned me into a registered nurse doing healing work that has changed lives. He has taken my feelings of brokenness, shame, and loneliness, and molded me into a woman who provides a sacred safe space for others who are passing through where I have been.

When I'm in front of a patient or any woman who feels afraid, depressed, or alone in the world, I can provide what she needs to feel better because I have been there. God can use our messiness to help others. None of our past was in vain. He uses my challenges to give other women hope.

I'm a living example that nothing at all is too big for God. He will give us the desires of our hearts. This I know. Yes, I sometimes experience waves of sadness. One day, that will be a thing of the past as well. The difference today is, I know how to care for myself, and I know where and with whom to rest my head and my soul.

Have faith in God's word and act on His direction. In this, we will always be well. And when He delivers us, we have a chance to share our journey to help others. Share freely with no shame attached. We are blessed and highly favored. Our steps are ordered. Everything in our path has a divine purpose. Be still and He will show you how to open your hands and heart and receive your beauty for ashes.

About the Authors

Dawn Baldwin Gibson serves as the executive pastor at Peletah Ministries, the church she and her husband, Pastor Anthony Gibson, founded in 2011. She is the mother of Spencer, Hannah, and Kaitlyn; the grandmother of Phillip; and daughter of Marva Fisher-Baldwin and the late Spencer L. Baldwin.

Gibson earned her liberal studies degree at Shaw University and her master's degree in English with a concentration in technical and professional communication from East Carolina University. She has nearly twenty years in collegiate education.

As an activist, Gibson is committed to community outreach. Recently, she was awarded the Humanitarian Award by the Craven County NAACP and was recognized by *My New Bern Magazine* as one of five women "Rising Leaders." She is also a certified HIS Christian Coach and the author of *A Place Called Home*, a chronicle of her family's 250 year history in North Carolina.

Learn more at www.dawnbaldwingibson.com.

Roz Knighten-Warfield is known as a smiling prayer warrior who creates power connections amongst women who desire to lead lives of execution, elevation, and empowerment. She is a certified power coach through Coach Academy International and shares writings with other women of influence such Dr. Anna McCoy and Thelma Wells. Her first devotional, *#StopIt & SMILE: Simply Make Intentional Love Encounters*, teaches ways to dismiss lower nature thinking that causes negativity. She has been an honored guest on TBN Tulsa KDOR-17 and has performed workshops promoting SMILE.

Knighten-Warfield is married to Vincent Warfield, who is affectionately known as her BOO (Beloved Only One). They have three children and one grandchild, and reside in Oak Cliff, Texas.

Learn more at www.stopitsmile.com.

Redina Thorpe Thomas was born in Savannah, Georgia. She is the mother of three, grandmother of three, a champion of women's rights, a feminist, and an educator who has worked with the public school system for twenty-five years. In addition to earning a bachelor of arts in English and a master's in education, she also holds middle grade, special education, and leadership certifications. She is a two-time Teacher of the Year nominee, Special Education Teacher of the year nominee, and a member of Phi Lamba International Honor Society.

Thorpe Thomas decided to let her voice be heard by ministering to woman who may not have found their inner voice. Her motto is "Never settle for less. God has adorned you for greatness, so go into the world and be great all for His Glory!"

Contact her at Ms.Redina.Thomas@gmail.com.

Tneshela Boyd-Jones, a native of Los Angeles, is a mother of two, entertainment consultant of twenty-five years, and a real estate professional. Realizing and re-considering her life's direction, she regrouped and set out to become an expert in the field of personal growth and development. As a coach and author, she offers tools to achieve specific goals and assists in overcoming personal obstacles, so that clients may operate at their highest level and their success becomes limitless.

Learn more at www.projectcelebrityent@gmail.com.

Donna Hicks Izzard is an author, speaker, technology executive, and minister. Her work centers on giving individuals the tools they need to move forward in all aspects of their lives, including personal, career, and business matters. She, along with former White House Ambassador Susan D. Johnson Cook, developed a strategy to touch as many lives as possible to women in ministry and business. This strategy is now the driving force behind Izzard's appearances in numerous conferences and seminars such as the Hampton Minister's Conference, which attracts tens of thousands of people. For her work, she received the Woman of Excellence Award from the Reverend Al Sharpton's National Action Network.

Izzard can be reached at www.donnaizzard.com.

Bonita Patton-Loggins was born and raised in Fort Worth, Texas. She is married to her childhood sweetheart, Patrick, with whom she has three beautiful children and five gorgeous grandchildren. She worked for XTO Energy/Exxon Mobil for nineteen years as a lease analyst and currently works for The Caffey Group as an independent land contractor.

Having a heart for God and people, Patton-Loggins volunteers at several non-profit organizations. Her passions are writing, uplifting, encouraging, and sharing God's love. Her motto, "Be the Unique You," formed after many years of realizing that she could love and place herself first. She stands tall and strong today in her faith that one can overcome anything with God.

Contact her at bonitaploggins@gmail.com.

Tilda Whitaker has mentored and coached hundreds to achieve their life purpose through P4 Coaching Institute, her nationally and internationally recognized 501c3 nonprofit organization. She trains extensively to help leaders plan, process, and produce with purpose to create legacies globally. Her message is set to compel the attention of those who seek to discover their purpose in life and launch their destinies.

In 2017, she will receive her accreditation by the International Coach Federation (ICF) as a Professional Certified Coach (PCC). She is a present ICF member, Pastor of Soul Winners International Ministries (SWIM), and author of *Essence of God's Joy*.

Becky Carter is an author, entrepreneur, leader, and mentor who offers career coaching and personal development to individuals who wish to put their best foot forward. A graduate of University of Texas, Arlington, she acquired a bachelor of science degree in business administration, and is now partner/co-owner for two businesses, A&B Creations, LLC., a design and décor company for special events, and Carter Properties, LLC., a landscape and lawn service company.

Next to serving God and His people, Carter's passions are in health, wellness, and self-care. She places deep emphasis on the importance of maintaining a healthy lifestyle through exercise and food choices. In doing so, she ministers to the masses about how the body is a temple and one must always "flex their faith.".

Tabitha Wright-Polote is a mother to one daughter, wife of twenty years, and woman of God. She received the Job of Excellence from President Barrack Obama for the Homeowners Assistance Award in the displacement and base realignments and closures of our servicemen and women. She is a graduate of Hampton University with a bachelor of arts in biology. She is a walking spiritual movement for God.

Wright-Polote may be reached via p.tabitha22@gmail.com.

Venessa D. Abram, a native of Gary, Indiana, is the wife of twenty-two-years to Anthony Sr. and the mother of three children. After earning her master of business administration degree with a focus in human resources management, she went on to become a best-selling Amazon author for her book, *Self Discovery. A Daily Journey*. The contents of the book was birthed from a myriad of life experiences that resulted in her rededication to God that created repositioning and self-discovery.

Her organization, Self-Discovery. A Daily Journey with Venessa, was birthed in December 2015. The mission of her movement is to inspire, empower, and coach souls to walk boldly into their purpose and be set apart. Her focal areas are brand building, personal and professional etiquette, grant writing, motivational speaking, interview preparation, dressing for success, and development of strengths via utilization of gifts and talents.

Learn more at www.venessaabram.com.

Shawna D. Brackens is an international award-winning speaker, author, educator, speech coach, and humanitarian. She has traveled to twenty-five nations as well as the forty-eight contiguous United States. She is the President of The Potter's House Fellowship International, and the Founder of The W.H.E.W. Global Platform and A Piece of Bread, Inc.

She is a graduate of Indiana University and is a certified T.E.S.O.L instructor. Her honors include The Rosa Parks Award, Outstanding Educator of the Year, and Korea Toastmasters National Speech Evaluation Champion. Her book, *Keep the Beat: The Rhythm of an Award-Winning Speech*, focuses on speech development and delivery.

She is currently living her dream of being a self-supported servant in East Asia. Her goal in life is to be an example of the believer in word, hope, and charity.

She welcomes your comments at soblessed777@yahoo.com

Taneisha Mitchell is a bestselling author of *After the Affair... What's Next?* She is also a speaker who advocates domestic violence awareness, forward-focused thinking, and movement of one's heart from brokenness and resentment to healing and restoration.

As a registered nurse, Mitchell knows how much healthy relationships and emotions play in our overall health. She is the owner and CEO of A+ Healthcare Partners Home Health Agency, which focuses on decreasing morbidity and mortality across underserved communities.

As a newly saved Christian, she turned her twenty-five-year long battle with feelings of unworthiness, abuse, and lack of loving with a shielded heart to building her personal relationship with God, which has led to newfound freedom and transformations.

Kim Francis graduate of University of North Texas who has over eighteen-years experience in television, media, and film marketing. She has produced numerous events within the telecommunications, sports, and non-profit industries. Most recently, she was the director affiliate marketing for AXS TV, HDNet Movies, and Magnolia Pictures, before taking a sabbatical to be with her mother who was battling esophageal cancer. Since then, she started the 1911 Media Marketing Consulting Group.

Francis hosts "The Empower Hour," a weekly radio show with Alliance 4 The Brave on 620AM KEXB in Dallas, Texas, and is an Amazon best-selling author in *Shift Happens: Inspirational Stories on Finding Happiness, Achieving Success & Overcoming Obstacles*. She serves as vice president of fundraising for the USA Film Festival, In addition, she is passionate in educating others about the warning signs of toxic black mold and esophageal cancer.

Connect at Break The Mold on Facebook or klfrancis2000@yahoo.com.

Denise Polote-Kelly is a business owner and founder of Winston H. Kelly, Sr. Memorial Foundation and Laps for Life. She is a two-time bestselling author and number one bestselling author of *God Loaned Me An Angel*, in which she shares her truth of God's love and her fight to live in hope and power after the death of her husband.

Polote-Kelly is a grief recovery specialist who assists in the healing of the grieving widows, widowers, and people who suffer loss of many kinds. She believes that grief is real and how we work through the grief determines how we will live through life. She teaches that we must live victoriously through all that we are challenged with and trust God in the process.

Polote-Kelly is a mother and grandmother. She resides in Savannah, Georgia.

Alexandria L. Barlowe was born and raised in Omaha, Nebraska. She graduated from Creighton University with a bachelor of science in entrepreneurial management in 2010. She published her first book, *No Good Thing,* in 2013, and has also worked as contributing editor for TheRichest.com.

Barlowe now resides in Dallas, Texas with her husband, James. They welcomed their first child, Vivian, in August 2016. She is now a freelance writer and work-at-home wife and mom. She is also a member of the Christian Women in Media Association.

She enjoys blogging, cooking, writing, and motherhood. In the future, she plans to have more children, further her writing career, and eventually own a salon and spa.

Learn more at AlexBarlowe.com.

Deandra D. Pritchett is on a mission by God to be instrumental in the lives of others. She is an elementary educator, youth advocate, speaker, and entrepreneur. She also serves in various capacities within her area to support local youth. She graduated from Dallas Christian College with a bachelor's degree in business administration and is currently pursuing her graduate studies in marriage and family counseling at Liberty University.

Pritchett believes that true change starts on the inside of each and every one of us. She resides in Dallas, Texas with her husband and three daughters.

Connect with Deandra on FB: www.facebook.com/deandrapritchett

Connect with Deandra at deandrapritchett@gmail.com.

Yolanda Williams is a speaker, coach, author, and pastor of Discipleship Services at Faithful Central Bible Church in Inglewood, California. As CEO of YolandaKaye Enterprises, LLC, she is passionate about helping leaders make their professional and entrepreneurial goals a reality. With over twenty years' experience in human resources and administration, Williams has trained leaders to successfully increase their productivity and set and achieve personal and professional goals through coaching, training seminars, and workshops. She is also a contributing author in *In Bloom Women's Devotion* and *Aspire! The New Women of Color Study Bible*.

A passionate and captivating speaker, Williams is a graduate of Hampton University and a member of Alpha Kappa Alpha Sorority, Inc. Married for twenty-seven years to her childhood sweetheart, Varick Williams, she is the proud mother of two amazing young adults, Kayla and Nicholas.

Learn more at www.yolandakaye.com.

Regina M. Poole is a native of Cincinnati, Ohio. She attended Ohio State University, Tuskegee University, and Cincinnati State where she majored in biology, ultrasound technology, and African American literature, respectively. In fall 2003, she made her theatre-acting debut as Sister Margaret in The Cincinnati Black Theatre's rendition of "The Amen Corner" by Ralph Ellison.

In 2013, Poole accepted a full-time position at the Office of Admission as an admissions recruiter at Cincinnati State Technical and Community College. She received the President's Award of Excellence from Dr. Odell Owens for her engagement in the community and commitment to continuing education for adult learners.

In January 2016, Poole began her national speaking tour "Meeting In The Ladies Room," which brings women together for transformative dialogue and networking centralized around faith, self-esteem, career empowerment, love and relationships, self care, and mental health.

Poole currently resides with her family in Jacksonville, Florida.

Pethral Daniels is an award-winning business owner of a human resources consulting firm in Atlanta, Georgia. She earned her bachelor's degree in human resources and her master's degree in organizational leadership from Mercer University. She is a certified HR professional and has become a highly sought-after resource for organizations of all sizes for her ability to offer transformational solutions. Her high-energy demeanor and passion for relationship building has accelerated her to being one of the best in her field.

Daniels is a mother of two and the grandmother of five, but most importantly, she prides herself on being a child of The King. She believes that her calling is to empower and help women have a relationship with God.

Sonya A. McKinzie is a resident of Lawrenceville, Georgia, where she resides with her beautiful six-year-old daughter. She is a Christian, mother, survivor of domestic violence, philanthropist, mentor, aspirant speaker, and the founder and executive director of Women of Virtue Transitional Foundation Inc., a 501(c)(3) nonprofit and charitable organization based in Duluth, Georgia. Her passion for helping victims of domestic violence is fueled by her relationship with God and the direct impact that domestic violence has had on her life. Her second book, *PERFECTLY IMPERFECT: Moving Above and Beyond the Pain*, was written for domestic violence victims and survivors to help with healing.

McKinzie uses her love for God and life experiences to pour into those who she comes in contact with. Her God-given purpose is to educate, empower, and encourage victims and struggling survivors to move towards living healthy, independent, and violence-free lives!

To connect, email her at womenofvirtuefoundation@gmail.com

M. Nichole Peters is a bestselling author, international motivational speaker, and founder of Women of Love, Power, and Respect and Believe In Your Dreams Productions. She is the producer of The Motivational Lounge, a TV/radio show powered by RHG Media and VoiceAmerica.

Peters was born and raised in Bogalusa, Louisiana. She is a diehard advocate for domestic violence survivors, who she reminds are beautiful, strong, and can live off true love, not abuse.

Kim Renee Samuels is founder of Image of Excellence Consulting firm, which offers motivational speaking, project management, coaching, and consulting. Kim has always believed that attitude is everything. She was diagnosed with lupus and has been an advocate for twenty-five years. Kim is also a minister and professional speaker who connects in a very down-to-earth style of speaking with her audiences by sharing real-life stories and presentations that the audience can relate to.

Kim has earned a bachelor's degree in computer science, an MBA, and a PMP. Through working in foreign missions and traveling to countries as a missionary, Kim lives out her desire to serve others and be a godly woman of excellence. She and her husband lead couple's ministry at Mt. Carmel Baptist Church, and she serves on the Board of Chesapeake Behavioral Healthcare and as minister/spiritual leader for A+ Healthcare Partners.

To learn more, visit her website at www.imageofexcellence.net

Doretta Gadsden is a registered nurse, speaker, best-selling author of *Living Victoriously: Strategies to Empower Women with a Chronic Diagnosis*, and a graduate of Bronx Community College. She has lived with AIDS for over twenty-five years and has a passion for serving women who are also challenged with a chronic diagnosis. She hosts workshops and works in her private coaching practice, empowering women in group settings with the knowledge that they are bigger than any diagnosis they may receive. Her mission is to teach women that they have a choice in defining what a diagnosis means to them.

Gadsden lives in Brooklyn, New York with her husband of twenty-one years.

Contact her at Info@womenwillbloom.com.

Cheryl Polote-Williamson is a transformational speaker, certified life coach, multi-bestselling author, and visionary entrepreneur. As the founder and CEO of Cheryl PW Speaks LLC, she helps female entrepreneurs build business and personal relationships based on honesty, integrity, and trust. Through her transparent and direct style, Cheryl helps women around the globe affirm their God-given skills and abilities.

A member of the Forbes Coaches Council and Christian Women in Media, Cheryl tours nationally to share her highly sought-after expertise in business development, providing positive and tangible solutions to other female entrepreneurs who are ready to grow and succeed. Her ability as a speaker to encourage, captivate, and empower audiences, along with her devotion to helping people walk out in their gifts, has earned her numerous awards, including the Chocolate Social Award for best online community, the Dallas Top 25 Award, and the Female Success Factor Award in 2016.

As a prolific author, and current nominee of the 2017 Indie Author Legacy Awards, Cheryl has published multiple books, including *Soul Reborn, Words from the Spirit for the*

Spirit, Safe House, Affirmed, Soul Talk, Soul Bearer, Soul Source, and is currently in the works to publish *Success Factor* and *Souled Out.*

Cheryl and her husband of twenty-five years, Russell, currently reside in Flower Mound, Texas, where they are members of St. John's Church Unleashed. They have three beautiful children, Russell Jr., Lauren, and Courtney, as well as an adorable granddaughter, Leah. In her spare time, Cheryl enjoys traveling, reading, serving others, and spending quality time with family and friends.

To learn more, visit her website at www.cherylpwspeaks.com

Sources

Unless otherwise indicated, scripture quotations are from the Holy Bible, King James Version. All rights reserved.

Scriptures marked ESV are taken from English Standard Version®. Copyright © 2001 by Crossway, a publishing ministry of Good News Publishers. All rights reserved.

Scriptures marked MSG are taken from The Message®. Copyright © 1993, 1994, 1995, 1996, 2000, 2001, 2002. Used by permission of NavPress Publishing Group.

Scriptures marked NASB are taken from the New American Standard Bible®. Copyright © 1960, 1962, 1963, 1968, 1971, 1972, 1973, 1975, 1977, 1995 by The Lockman Foundation. Used by permission.

Scriptures marked NIV are taken from the New International Version®. Copyright © 1973, 1978, 1984, 2011 by Biblica, Inc.™. All rights reserved.

Scriptures marked NLT are taken from the New Living Translation®. Copyright © 1996, 2004, 2007, 2013 by Tyndale House Foundation. All rights reserved.

CREATING DISTINCTIVE BOOKS WITH INTENTIONAL RESULTS

We're a collaborative group of creative masterminds with a mission to produce high-quality books to position you for monumental success in the marketplace.

Our professional team of writers, editors, designers, and marketing strategists work closely together to ensure that every detail of your book is a clear representation of the message in your writing.

Want to know more?
Write to us at info@publishyourgift.com
or call (888) 949-6228

Discover great books, exclusive offers, and more at
www.PublishYourGift.com

Connect with us on social media

@publishyourgift